DON'T DRINK THE KOOLAIDE

Dear Karen,

It was such a pleasure to meet you and hear your message. You are someone special in our industry you are real and authentic! That's hard to find these days.

Thank you for the gifts. Please let me know how my team and I can support you on your journey.

Keep Making It Happen!

2019

DON'T DRINK THE KOOLAIDE

A Guide To Live Life on Your Terms

Bert Oliva

Printed in the United States of America

First Printing, 2017

ISBN-13: 978-1548538071

ISBN-10: 1548538078

Make It Happen Publishing
12235 SW 129th Court
Miami, FL 33186

1-888-711-2044

This book is dedicated to my wife, Alexandra, my children, Myles, Sabrina, and Dylan, and to my team, Valerie and Eric. It has been a work 23 years in the making and has been a sincere collaboration. Most of all, this book is dedicated to my mother, Victoria, who spent her life giving me the best she could and always taught me to share my views with the world.

Table of Contents

Author's Preface	1
How to Use This Book	6
Introduction	11
Chapter 1: The Walking Dead	14
Chapter 2: Squirrel Effect	29
Chapter 3: I Am Special	40
Chapter 4: The Secret to Happiness	53
Chapter 5: Identity Crisis	64
Chapter 6: Human Connection	76
Chapter 7: The Forbidden Topic	88
Conclusion	104
Notes Section	106
Appendix	121
Glossary	123
Index	128

AUTHOR'S PREFACE

I love the brain. The brain is more powerful than any super computer and studies have shown we only use 10 percent of our brain capacity, at most. There is so much potential power within our minds and ourselves, but we so often allow ourselves to be numbed out of thinking. It almost seems like constant stimulation is causing desensitization in all aspects of our life. This book is meant as a wake-up call for all of us.

Human Behavior

I am so passionate about human behavior because it is one of the most complex things for us to understand. I love researching, experiencing, and learning about various methods that can increase our brain function while providing us the ability to live a substantial quality of life.

I am also so passionate about human behavior because of so many different relationships—some successful and some failed—that I have encountered in my life. I still want to understand the dynamics of where I went wrong in failed relationships and compare them to where I went right in the successful ones. I truly feel that if each of us takes time for this type of introspection, we could help to improve all of our relationships overall.

Communication Is Key

Everything comes down to communication, whether we are communicating with others or even with ourselves. And communication has dramatically changed in just the last decade with the increased use of technology. I can go days now without speaking to someone on the telephone but will have communicated via email and text with more people in that same time frame than I used to in an entire two-week period. Technology is amazing, but we're becoming even less fluent in human-to-human communication every day that we allow ourselves to become isolated.

We are all known to speak one main language. It is said that we are considered to be fluent in our native language when we know between 20,000 and 40,000 words in that language. However, 93 percent of our communication is nonverbal. It is time for us to become fluent in the way we use our words, bodies, technology, and even minds to communicate with others and ourselves. It is time for us to stop living and communicating so much of our lives unconsciously. It is time to wake up.

Goal of this Book

This book is designed to shock people out of their comfort zones to realize how much of their lives are on autopilot. In order to achieve true contentment in our lives, we must be in full control of our own minds, choices, and actions. We must live life on our own terms.

As a society we now love to blame other people for the problems that really lie within ourselves as an individual. We need to stop the self-inflicting negativity and focus on the things that truly make us content. The problem is that we are so bombarded with all the negativity every time we look around that we get lost.

One of the purposes I have in sharing this book is that you open your eyes and realize that change happens with you and you have the power to affect those around you in a positive or negative way. I am hoping you choose the positive and that ripple of positivity is what starts affecting our society.

Do Not Take My Word for It

As you read this book, you may be wondering if I am trying to get you to conform to my ways of thinking. I am not asking you to adhere to my methods and ways of thinking in any way, shape, or form. I am not asking you to blindly follow this book. The goal of this book is for you to make Rational Educated Decisions (RED) for yourself.

I am merely giving you examples I have used and have used with my students so that you can find something that fits the formula of your life. These recommendations are based on the thousands of hours of self-study, formal study, client coaching, and observations I have done over my career.

However, we are each unique, and the life recipes that work for each of us must be our own. My goal is to simply provide you with the knowledge of how your mind works so that you can find the right life recipe for yourself.

All this book is meant to do is help you to learn to take everything with a grain of salt and allow you to choose your reality. The goal is to have you move from blaming others to taking responsibility for how you live your life and how you affect the lives of those around you.

As with everything in life, this book is a work in progress. Please share with me your thoughts and experiences after reading it. And remember, everything you need to live a successful and content life is already within you. These words are simply one more way to hopefully wake up those parts within yourself.

Now go out and Make It Happen!

Live Life,

Bert Oliva
Miami, Florida
June 2017

HOW TO USE THIS BOOK

This book is written so that you can use it in multiple ways. You can read it straight through or you can choose a chapter that resonates with you and work on the techniques provided there.

Take Notes

I do suggest that you take notes and also write down any thoughts and feelings that may arise as you read. In the back of this book are some pages designed for note taking separated into sections for each chapter.

Write all over this book. Make it yours. This is also a great way to ensure that you take the knowledge you learn or confirm in this book and internalize it. Remember, 80 percent of retention comes from an action. So write things down!

Chapter Sections

Each chapter is broken up into multiple sections, including scenarios, negative definitions, case studies, positive definitions, and techniques.

Each of these will be explained further in the following paragraphs.

Scenarios

Each chapter begins with a scenario. It is meant to help you see how the chapter may relate to your life. Some scenarios are a little exaggerated to prove a point, but each is designed to be an engaging example of the subject for the chapter.

Imagine This: *This is a sample scenario...*

Negative Definitions

After each scenario, you will be presented with the definition of the negative aspect of the chapter as well as a more detailed explanation of the topic. These topics may be slightly different takes on terms you are familiar with, but I've chosen to use them to make this book both easily applicable as well as appealing to your mind. When your mind is presented with something it is not fully familiar with, it is more likely to pay attention.

NEGATIVE DEFINITION: THIS IS A SAMPLE ...

Case Studies

Next, you'll be presented with a Case Study. These Case Studies are based on actual students I have worked with; however, their names and some identifiable personal characteristics have been changed to protect their identity. Each Case Study shows how the negative topic in the chapter was affecting the person and then explains the steps we took together to change the situation.

Positive Definitions

Following each Case Study, you'll be given the positive definition of the topic the student developed. This section goes into detail on why the techniques we worked on actually helped make a difference in the student's life and how you can apply these techniques to your life.

Techniques

Finally, each chapter ends with additional techniques and tools you can use to develop the positive trait in your own life. Though each technique is designed to be as simple as possible, each is also extremely powerful when done correctly.

Additional Features

This book also includes numerous footnotes, a glossary, an index, and an appendix. Each of these are meant to make this book an easy access resource if you ever want to go back to review a topic quickly or want to be able to know where to find out more information.

INTRODUCTION

We're all brainwashed.[1] Yes, even you. More often than not, your reactions, emotional responses, and even thoughts have a basis in something subconscious. Throughout our lives we are conditioned by our upbringing, society, and experiences. This is not necessarily good or bad, but it's time to stop living unconsciously. It's time to become aware of the "Koolaide"[2] you are unconsciously drinking on a regular basis and start choosing what you want to think.

Negativity Bias

We have about 60,000 thoughts per day (one per second). About 95 percent of those thoughts are repeats from the day before and the day before that. Moreover, 80 percent of our thoughts are negative.

---

[1] Brainwashing actually began as a positive term in Chinese culture. The term was punned on the Taoist custom of "cleaning/washing the heart/mind."
[2] "Drinking the Koolaide" is a phrase commonly used in the United States to refer to someone who goes along with an idea because of peer pressure. The phrase has its origins in the Jonestown deaths of 1978 where over 900 followers of Jim Jones committed suicide by drinking poison combined with flavored drink mix.

That means we have around 45,000 negative thoughts per day.[3]

We are conditioned evolutionarily and societally speaking to be negative and to focus on the negative. This book is about recognizing that conditioning and reprogramming it for ourselves so that we are in the driver's seat of our own minds, thoughts, and actions.

Rational Educated Decisions (#IThinkRED)

In so much of our world today we take sound bites as fact. We do our research on Facebook and our decision-making based on tweets. Education is no longer valued here in the United States, but rather results are. Instead of ensuring that our children fully understand a concept and can use it to think for themselves, we are more concerned with them knowing how to perform on a standardized test so that our schools "rank" high. But all that ranking means is that our schools get more funding, not that our children are getting better educations. We are so focused on the results that we forget about working with each individual student to ensure they perform at the best of their abilities.

In our modern world where information is everywhere (to the point where we are almost

---

[3] Cleveland Clinic Wellness http://www.clevelandclinicwellness.com /programs/NewSFN/pages/default.aspx?Lesson=3&Topic=2&UserId=00000000-0000-0000-0000-000000000705

immune to it), being well educated is even more vital, but you have to take your education into your own hands. You need to be informed and know how to think for yourself. Do not just take anyone's word for anything. Research it from multiple sources, apply it to your own life, and see what works for you.

What is important is understanding how *you* work—so that you are not just on autopilot skating through life till one day you realize you missed out on truly living. That is what this book is about—becoming aware of your own tendencies and society's so that you live your life consciously—making your own choices of which you are completely aware. The goal of this book is to show you how to arm yourself with the knowledge, examples, and techniques necessary to stop drinking the Koolaide around you and start thinking RED. It is time to make Rational Educated Decisions for yourself.

Please use the hashtag #IThinkRED to share with us your thoughts and ideas on your own Rational Educated Decisions and join the conversation on social media.

CHAPTER 1

The Walking Dead

Imagine This: *Your alarm goes off at 6:30am. You hit the snooze button. You get up at 6:45am groaning. You go brush your teeth and wash your face. You get dressed for the day. You walk in the kitchen and do a double take as you read 8:15am on the wall clock. You're late. Where did all the time go? How does this make you feel? You grab your car keys and rush out the door. You yell at slow drivers as you sit in traffic. Finally you get to work and seem to just count the hours until 5pm. Then you rush out the office door, sit in your car in rush-hour traffic, finally get home, eat some dinner, and pass out while watching TV till your alarm goes off at 6:30am…*

The above scenario may not be exactly something you have experienced, but more than likely you have experienced, at least at one point or another in your life, some type of repetitive pattern that has led to your days seeming to run into each other, not knowing really when one day ends and another begins. This is the 9-5 mentality.

> <u>9-5 MENTALITY:</u> IN TODAY'S SOCIETY, WE HAVE THE ABILITY TO GET CAUGHT UP IN THE EVERYDAY ROUTINES OF LIFE, OR WHAT WE LIKE TO CALL THE "9-5 MENTALITY;" A.K.A. "THE VICIOUS CYCLE"

This does not necessarily mean that you clock in at 9am and clock out at 5pm but that you have a pattern of working and living that is concreting those processes in your daily living. Every day that you stay within these patterns makes it a stronger habit to break. This can also lead us to an autopilot method of thinking. If you have worked anywhere for a year or so, you have probably driven to work at some point without remembering that you drove there. You are on autopilot.

If we continue to live in a 9-5 mentality for an extended period of time, we eventually realize we are not happy. We start asking, "Is this what I have to do for the rest of my life?" We can find ourselves begrudgingly accepting these routines with justifications such as having to provide for our families, etc. However, after many years of living these routines, you can no longer snap out of it easily. You have become part of the "Walking Dead"—a zombie in your own life.

WALKING DEAD: A PERSON WHO MOVES VERY SLOWLY AND IS NOT AWARE OF WHAT IS HAPPENING ESPECIALLY BECAUSE OF BEING VERY TIRED; A PERSON HELD TO RESEMBLE THE SO-CALLED WALKING DEAD (A ZOMBIE); ESPECIALLY : AUTOMATON

AUTOMATON: A PERSON OR ANIMAL THAT ACTS IN A MONOTONOUS, ROUTINE MANNER, WITHOUT ACTIVE INTELLIGENCE

What's Going On

Patterns are comforting. Our brains like patterns. And we are creatures of routine. Some routines are helpful. A good morning routine can get us through our morning quickly, but living our entire lives on autopilot is not ideal.

If you wake up every day at the same time, brush your teeth the same way, get dressed the same way, maintain your morning, afternoon, and evening rituals every day, etc., you are programming your mind. You are actually "cementing" your memory and your habits.

Fair Warning

The next few paragraphs are going to get a bit scientific and technical. This is the only part of the book that will do that. I felt it was necessary in order to explain to you exactly how our brains work and why the techniques provided in each chapter are so effective. Please bear with me; I promise it is only a few pages and it is worth knowing. However, you can always choose to skip the next section and go right to the following one entitled "45 Seconds, 21 Days, 6 Months, 9 Years."

Brain "Cement"

You have probably heard the phrase, "You can't teach an old dog new tricks." That phrase has its origins in old beliefs and studies that suggested that our brains solidified as we got older and literally cemented and got set in stone. However, new studies have shown that our brains have a quality known as neuroplasticity, which in the simplest definition is the brain's ability to reorganize and change itself by forming new neural pathways throughout life. Basically, this means that our brains will create new connections due to changes in behavior, environment, neural processes, thinking, and emotions even in adulthood.

So if our brains are able to change all the time, then why are habits so hard to break? To understand this, we must understand the basic structure of our neurons, which are the building blocks of the brain.

Neurons receive information through dendrites and send information through axons. Dendrites and axons of different neurons communicate through synapses. The actual information that is passed along these pathways is electrical impulses.[4]

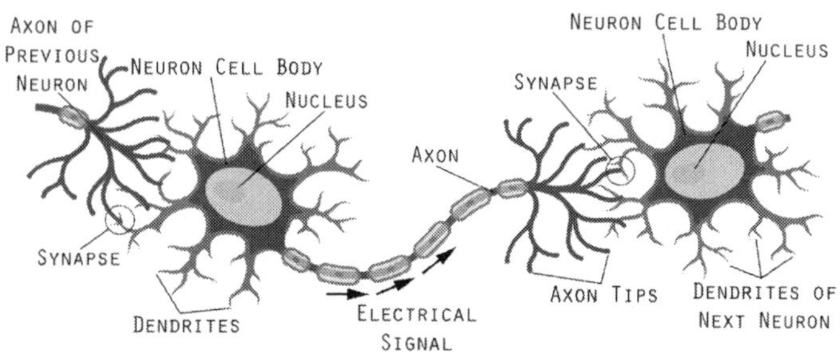

Basic Structure of Neurons

Now, the more often a certain neural pathway is used, two different things occur that make that neural pathway stronger. First of all, as a neural pathway becomes more active, a fatty tissue known as myelin begins to form around the axon, protecting loss of signal and increasing the speed of the signal as it travels from one neuron to another. This myelin is known as the "white matter" of the brain.

---

[4] Shen, Jason. "Why Practice Actually Makes Perfect: How to Rewire Your Brain for Better Performance." *Buffer Social.* Oct 15, 2014. https://blog.bufferapp.com/why-practice-actually-makes-perfect-how-to-rewire-your-brain-for-better-performance

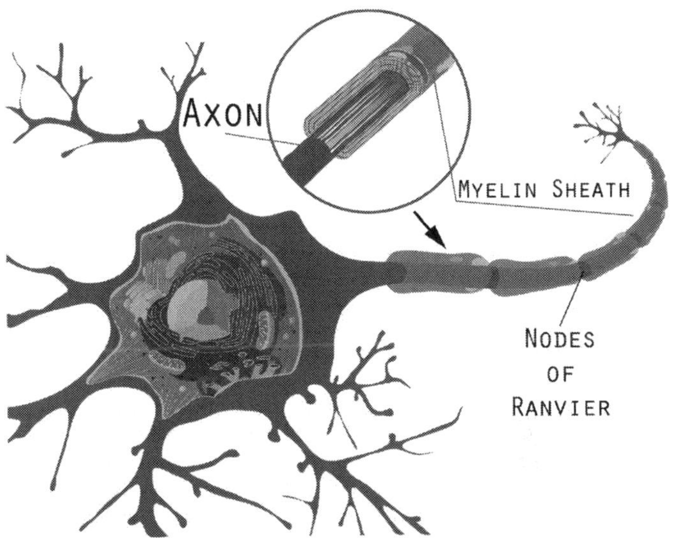

Myelin Sheath, a.k.a. "White Matter" of the Brain

Studies of musicians brains have shown the more they practice, the more "white matter" they have and the denser it will be in certain regions of their brains.[5] The importance of myelin can also be seen in such diseases as Parkinson's and Multiple Sclerosis, in which damage to myelin leads to blurry vision, loss of dexterity, general weakness, fatigue, and many other symptoms. Myelin production occurs more quickly in children, but it does still occur in adults as well.

---

[5] Bengtsson, Sara L, Zotan Nagy, Stefan Skare, Lea Forsman, Hans Forssbert, & Fredrik Ullen. "Extensive piano practicing has regionally specific effects on white matter development." *Nature Neuroscience.* Sept 2005. http://www. brainmusic.org/EducationalActivitiesFolder/Bengtsson_practicing2005.pdf

Secondly, the more often a synapse is used, the more neurotransmitter receptor sites are created. This process, known as Long-Term Potentiation (LTP), increases the speed and strengthens the efficacy of communication between two neurons. At the same time, synapses can be weakened through a process known as Long-Term Depression (LTD), which occurs when synapses are not used as much.

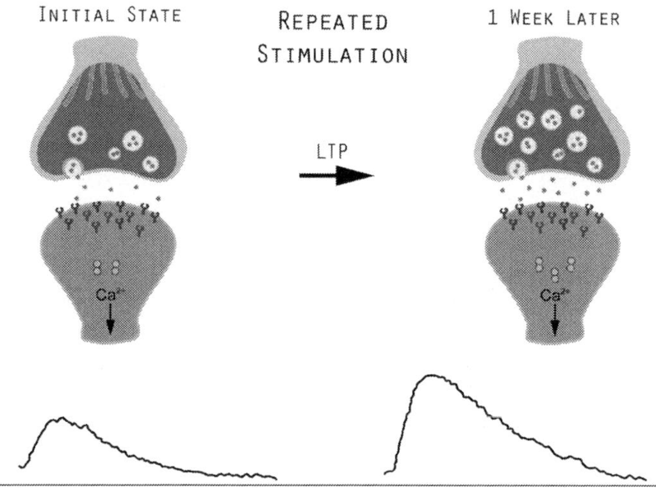

Number of Neurotransmitter Receptor Sites Increases with Repeated Stimulation

So, basically, the more you perform a certain action, think a certain thought, etc., the faster and more efficiently that signal will flow from one neuron to the other, in essence, making that neural pathway and train of thought that much stronger.

However, our brains do not differentiate between "good" trains of thoughts and patterns and "bad" ones. Our brains simply look to make our minds as efficient as possible and strengthen the neural pathways that get used the most. And because our brains like efficiency, they will choose the stronger neural pathway every time, if we let them. Thus, if you have been smoking for 20 years, your brain is more likely to choose the smoking neural pathway when you are stressed over the new gum chewing pathway you just started to build.

Notice the phrase in the previous paragraph. Our brains will choose the stronger neural pathway every time, *if we let them.* We truly have the ability to reprogram our minds at any point in our lives. We can learn to become aware of the habits and processes we do not like and create new ones. However, this takes time, dedication, and a lot of practice.

45 Seconds, 21 Days, 6 Months, 9 Years

Because of our brain's unique neuroplasticity, it really does not take very long to begin to change our habits and routines. In fact, it takes about 45 seconds to simply change our state—state of mind or state of being. That means, in 45 seconds time, you can actually change your mood if you truly focus on it.

Have you ever been in a really bad mood and then suddenly your favorite song comes on, you sing and dance to it for a few moments, and suddenly you are in a much better place? That is because you were able to completely change your state. Learning to change your state is the first step to learning how to get out of any type of rut. When you realize you truly are in control of how you feel right at this very moment, you will be amazed at the immense feeling of personal power that will come over you.

It takes at least 21 days to change or create a habit.[6] This process may take longer for habits that you have been performing for longer periods of time (the neural pathways are stronger), but in general, many people will at least begin to see a true change in their habits after 21 consecutive days of dedicated new behavior. This gives the new neural pathways time to strengthen and the older ones time to weaken a little bit.

However, remember, it took years to build the strong neural pathway of the habit you are trying to change, so it will take just as long to get the new neural pathway that strong. That is why awareness is vital during the process of habit change. You

---

[6] The 21-day observation was first made by Maxwell Maltz in his book *Psycho Cybernetics*. However, a 2009 study at University College in London has shown that habits can take as long as 66 or even 254 days to create or change. https://getmomentum.com/21-days-66-days-254-days/

must make conscious decisions to fight your easy neural paths and choose new behaviors.

I have observed that in six months' time, you will create an addiction. This is neither necessarily good nor bad, but if you have performed a certain behavior consistently for six months and then choose to stop the behavior, you will more than likely have a physical reaction to it. For instance, if you go to the gym every day to workout for six months, and then you miss a day, you will probably feel physically sick or fatigued.

Finally, we become institutionalized at nine years. More than likely that word brings up the idea of prison to you, but that is not what it means here. In this usage, it means after doing a certain behavior after nine years, the chances of us breaking that behavior is greatly reduced. For instance, people who have been married for over nine years are much less likely to get divorced. Just like people who have been in a specific career for over nine years are much less likely to change jobs.

The same can be observed with nearly every aspect in your life. When you have been doing the same routine and behaviors and having the same thought processes for over nine years, it is much harder for you to have new independent thought processes in that situation. It is by no means impossible, because our brains are amazing, but it will definitely take immense dedication on your part.

Case Study: Margaret

Great. So you just learned how your brain really works and how long it takes to create change within yourself, but what does that really mean? I truly believe that knowledge is not power, but potential power. It's what you do with it that makes a difference. So let's take a look at a case study of one of my students, Margaret.

Margaret was a coaching client who had a problem with so many negative thoughts that it was driving her into a depression. Her standard inner monologue went something like this: *"I'm no good. Why are other people so successful? I'm such a loser. I must have done something seriously bad in my previous life and I'm paying for it now."*

She was on the verge of taking anti-depressants when she came to me. Now, let me just state here that I don't disagree with the use of anti-depressants. These medications are a tool that can be very useful depending on the situation. However, I do believe that a lot of times we tend to go straight for the "easy" medicinal "fix," rather than first trying to work with the power of our own minds.

Because Margaret had never had a history of depression before and she was in a very stable environment, I suggested that she try a method of state change for a few weeks before she tried the medication. Every time she caught herself having a negative thought she would sing the song “Don’t Worry, Be Happy” by Bobby McFerrin. Sometimes she would sing the song in her head, other times she would sing it aloud to drown out the negative thoughts.

Over the first 21 days, the more she sang the song the less she even thought of the negative things. Today, she now knows how to maintain a more positive thinking pattern.

Why did this work so well for Margaret? Because the song had a strong, positive emotional tie for her. Emotions, like taking actions, help to cement a neural pathway. If there is no action or emotion, it is much harder for you to recall the details of something (that is, create stronger neural pathways). With Margaret, we used both emotion and action. The emotion came in with the song she loved; the action came in when she physically sang it in her mind or out loud.

We chose this song because it was a positive anchor for Margaret, but just about anything can be used in this method. You can use a word, a rubber band to snap on your wrist, or even a permanent marker spot on your forehead. All of these things help you do one thing: create awareness of your subconscious thought patterns and behaviors. I have recommended many of these methods to my clients over the years for anything from negative thinking, to unconscious bad language, and even overeating.

Affirmative Conditioning

This method is actually something known as Affirmative Conditioning.

> AFFIRMATIVE CONDITIONING: SELF-THINKING; THINKING FOR ONE'S SELF; FORMING ONE'S OWN OPINIONS, AND NOT BORROWING THEM READY-MADE FROM OTHERS, OR MERELY FOLLOWING PREVALENT FASHIONS OF THOUGHT; OR INDEPENDENT JUDGMENT

> CONDITIONING: THE ACT OR PROCESS OF TRAINING A PERSON OR ANIMAL TO DO SOMETHING OR TO BEHAVE IN A CERTAIN WAY IN A PARTICULAR SITUATION

By becoming aware of our patterns and applying positive affirmative actions to counteract these patterns, we are able to reprogram ourselves from the 9-5 mentality to one of personal awareness and power. This is why our minds are such incredible tools; we have everything within ourselves to change just about any habit, pattern, or routine we want.

Affirmative conditioning encourages a happier state of mind and studies have shown that when you feel happier, you attract better results, and can even prolong your life.

More Techniques

In order to effectively use affirmative conditioning, you first must figure out which habits or patterns that you want to break or change. Remember to start slowly, by focusing on just one thing. If you set your goal too wide, you set yourself up for failure before you even begin.

As shown with Margaret, music can be an excellent tool for changing your state.[7] Starting your day off with a powerful song can set the tone for your entire day. However, make sure that you research the lyrics of the song, as lyrics can subconsciously program our minds if we are not aware of what is being said.

Visualization is another excellent affirmative conditioning technique. Visualize your life once this habit or pattern has been changed. What will be different? How will you feel? How will you describe your life? Engage as many of your senses

---

[7] Music is one of the few activities that involves using the whole brain. It is intrinsic to all cultures and can have surprising benefits not only for learning language, improving memory, and focusing attention, but also on physical coordination and development; research has shown that music can decrease the amount of cortisol, a stress-related hormone produced by the body in response to stress. http://www.emedexpert.com/tips/music.shtml

as you can. Whenever you become aware that you are performing the habit you want to break, pause and perform this visualization technique for a few minutes. This type of visualization/meditation will help you cultivate an appreciation of your life and help build a strong connection between the new habit and this positive feeling, which will make it easier for you to create the new pattern.

Awareness Is Freedom

How you live your life is completely your choice. You can continue to live as a part of the Walking Dead. There is absolutely nothing wrong with it; the choice is yours. This is simply a call for you to become aware of your choices. Stop blaming society, circumstances, and others for where you are in your life. Happiness, choice, and freedom start within your own mind. You truly hold all the power.

CHAPTER 2

Squirrel Effect

Imagine This: *This morning your boss asks you to write a quick report summarizing the progress of your latest project. As you begin to write, you realize you need to know how to spell a certain word. You do a quick Internet search. While you are searching, a notification pops up for an email from an old friend wanting to reconnect. You search for your friend on your favorite social media platform. There you see your mom posted a picture from her vacation. You reach out to your mom via text telling her you love her. She decides to call you to give you an update on her trip. You step outside to talk to her for a few minutes. When you come back to your desk, you realize an hour and a half has gone by. Then you notice you still do not know how to spell that word and do another Internet search, only to be distracted by an ad telling you about a one-day sale...*

The above scenario may not be completely accurate for your life, but odds are that you have definitely found yourself pulled in multiple directions at once only to discover after an extended period of time that you have not accomplished the one task you had originally set out to do in the first place. This lack of focus is something I like to call the "Squirrel Effect"[8] or "Attention Deficit."

> ATTENTION DEFICIT: A DISORDER IN WHICH SOMEONE (SUCH AS A CHILD) HAS PROBLEMS WITH LEARNING AND BEHAVIOR BECAUSE OF BEING UNABLE TO THINK ABOUT OR PAY ATTENTION TO THINGS FOR VERY LONG; A.K.A. "SQUIRREL EFFECT"

This definition probably brings to mind the terms "ADD" or "ADHD," Attention Deficit Disorder or Attention Deficit Hyperactive Disorder, respectively. However, in today's modern world where we are utterly overstimulated and asked to multitask to the nth degree, we all suffer from some form of attention deficit or another at least from time to time.

In fact, oftentimes now, "ADD" tends to be an excuse for people. *"I can't focus. I have ADD." "My ADD is kicking in right now..."* We are all so

---

[8] The "Squirrel Effect" refers to the Disney Pixar movie *Up*, in which the dog characters are continuously distracted at the mention of squirrels.

quick to label ourselves and give ourselves excuses as to why we are feeling overwhelmed. Most of us even try to get four to five things done at once and become frustrated when we get stuck.

ADD is a medical disorder, but odds are that you do not have ADD to the point of needing medication. Truly, anything in this book can be diagnosed as a disorder, self-diagnosed, or used as an excuse. Making excuses is the easier route. *"I'm just sick. I don't have to change. Just feel sorry for me."*

Focus Is Key

It may not seem like lack of focus is too big of a problem, but it can interfere with your workday and every aspect of your life. Having your mind wander into areas that will not allow you to finish anything can be exasperating. It can even move into a state of laziness or not feeling like you can wake up without caffeine. One of the worst things about having a lack of concentration is that it can lead to burnout. And when you are burnt out you can alienate yourself from others, become a danger when you are driving or using machinery, increase your stress hormones, or even become depressed.

Focus is the key to success in anything. We need a driving point or destination. If you do not have a focus for the next year, or even just the next 10 minutes, before you know it, 10 years can go by.

When you have a focus or goal, you work toward something. According to metaphysical laws, such as the law of attraction, when you put energy and keen focus on what you want—when you want something badly—you tap into a whole different realm. And believe it or not, focus is a skill you can learn just like anything else.

Causes of Attention Deficit

Our lack of focus can sometimes be attributed to different factors like nutritional deficiencies, lack of sleep, or other medical issues. Oftentimes our overuse of technology with its hundreds of different notifications can be the culprit. You just need to recognize, truly look at, and analyze yourself to figure out what is really contributing to your lack of focus.

Case Study: Chase

I want to share with you Chase, a client in his early 20s that I had a couple of years ago, who had diagnosed himself as having ADD. After careful observation of his daily routine, I found that he always used the excuse that he could not focus whenever he became bored with a daily task. He was always really excited with new projects, but whenever he got to the middle of them or they became mundane, he would lose focus and do something he enjoyed more, such as texting his girlfriend. Thus, tasks that should take minimal time would take him days to complete and he would not even complete them well.

I told Chase my analysis and asked him point blank what he wanted to do. Did he want to go to a mental health professional, get tested for ADD, and go on medication? Or did he want to tap into the power of his mind? I told him that I thought the former option was an excuse and the easy way out for him. He did not have ADD, because his attention and focus only swayed when he got bored or had an uninteresting task to do. It was not a consistent problem that he was having, but rather a lack of focal development. Chase agreed to give some mental focusing techniques a try.

I had Chase use a time sheet for a week. From the time he woke up to the time he went to bed each day, he recorded what he did every hour. When he returned to me after the week, he came with a time sheet that was only half filled out. He said he forgot to fill out when he changed tasks or when time had passed by. I had him go back for another week, but this time with a 15-minute timer set on his phone during working hours. Every time the timer went off, he had to take a moment and record what he was doing in his time sheet. When he came back for his weekly session he was amazed; he saw in his own handwriting how often he changed focus mid task.

The following week, I had Chase do a daily to-do list, along with his time sheet tracking and 15-minute timer. Every morning, before he started his day, he listed every task he had to do and then prioritized them. He then took the top three and put them on a separate list and put the larger list away. I had him do this because Chase, like many people with attention deficit, tend to be very high achievers in their minds. They create long to-do lists with lofty goals of achieving all of them within a matter of minutes, when in reality, even if they were able to fully focus, they would not be able to complete even a tenth of the tasks on the list. Having long to-do lists tend to overwhelm our subconscious minds, and when we are overwhelmed, we tend to want to avoid everything we have to do altogether. By limiting Chase to three tasks at a time, he had an attainable list he could work on that was not scary.

After that, he would choose the first priority task on the list and simply focus on that until it was finished. Every time his 15-minute timer would go off, if he had stayed focused on the one task throughout the time he would take a two to three-minute break. This break could be anything from texting his girlfriend to getting a cup of coffee, but the break could not be longer than two to three minutes. Because of Chase's tendency for losing track of time, I had him set a second timer on his phone for these breaks. On his fourth consecutive 15-minute work span on the same task, he took a longer 10-15 minute break. This break could be used for leaving his desk and stretching his legs, making a personal call, or anything else. Yet again, his break could not be longer than the 10-15 minutes.

When Chase returned to me, after using this time management technique, he told me that he struggled at first. The first day he kept swaying from his singular task and barely got rewarded by any breaks. The second day he focused more and was able to achieve one 10-minute break for himself. By the end of the week, however, he had the technique working for him fully and was actually able to complete 50 percent of his task list, which was 50 percent more than he had been achieving prior to using the technique.

As time went on, we expanded Chase's work time periods to 25 minutes. Now Chase for the most part is able to fully focus on his tasks at hand and has even more free time to enjoy other things in his personal life.

What's Going On

The techniques used with Chase were all Focal Development tools.

<u>FOCAL DEVELOPMENT:</u> FOSTERING ATTENTION OR FOCUS

ATTENTION: THE ACT OR POWER OF CAREFULLY THINKING ABOUT, LISTENING TO, OR WATCHING SOMEONE OR SOMETHING; NOTICE, INTEREST, OR AWARENESS

FOCUS: A MAIN PURPOSE OR INTEREST

Time tracking allowed Chase to see in black and white how much he wasted time by trying to multitask. (A recent *Harvard Business Review* post said multitasking leads to as much as a 40 percent drop in productivity, increased stress, and a 10 percent drop in IQ.[9]) The timer forced Chase to focus and become aware of his actions. Finally the alternating between work and short breaks is based on the Pomodoro Technique, Francesco Cirillo's time management method he developed in the late 1980s.[10] This method is based on studies that have shown that regular breaks can improve mental agility and focus. The Pomodoro Technique is an excellent method for anyone who gets easily distracted, because the person knows they will get the reward after they finish each work period (or "pomodoro" as Cirillo called them).

---

[9] Bergman, P. "How (and Why) to Stop Multitasking." *Harvard Business Review*. May 20, 2010. https://hbr.org/2010/05/how-and-why-to-stop-multitaski.html

[10] The method gets its name from a tomato-shaped kitchen timer that Cirillo used with his students to measure their work intervals, which Cirillo called "pomodoros."

The Truth

Like Chase most of us do not have a lack of focus or ADD or any other label you want to call it. The truth is we suffer from the "Squirrel Effect" and are easily bored. Moreover, in our modern world it is too easy to choose to focus on the things that interest us and ignore the things that bore us. And now, with technology so readily available at our fingertips or even on our wrists, we can easily be distracted. With so many distractions we have to work even harder to cultivate focus.

Find Your Passion, Find Your Focus

When we realize our purpose and interest, it helps bring focus. This does not mean you have to find your "life's purpose" to find focus, but when you have a set goal in mind (like Chase's three tasks so he can text his girlfriend), you are more able to focus on achieving that goal. Few students in school enjoy doing homework, yet studies show that children in magnet programs outdo children in regular school settings.[11] Why? Because the students in the magnet programs are in programs that are specialized in something the students are interested in. Magnet students also have a higher graduation rate than students in normal high schools and even exhibit more positive attitudes toward

---

[11] "A Review of the Research on Magnet Schools." *Information Capsule: Research Services*. Vol 1105. Jan 2012. http://www.magnet.edu/files /documents/review-of-research-on-magnet-schools.pdf

their academics in general. When you find something to be passionate about (even if it is as simple as completing your daily to-do list so you can reward yourself with a cup of coffee), you enjoy your work more, do your work better, and often even complete it faster.

More Focal Development Techniques

As technology is one of the biggest distractions we have nowadays, try disconnecting for a set period of time once in a while. Go for a walk and leave your cell phone at home. Pay attention to the emotions being disconnected brings up. At first you may be a little anxious about missing someone's text or call, but before you know it, you will probably be enjoying the quiet and freedom of it.

Meditation is another excellent way to develop your focus. A study in the *Journal of Neuroscience* compares the brain scans of regular meditators to non-meditators. It shows that those who regularly meditate have the ability to quiet brain activity that is related to lack of concentration.[12] If you have never meditated before, guided meditations are a great way to start.

---

[12] Pagnoni G. "Dynamical Properties of BOLD Activity from the Ventral Posteromedial Cortex Associated with Meditation and Attentional Skills." *Journal of Neuroscience*. Apr 11 2012, 32(15):5242-9. http://www.jneurosci.org/content/32/15/5242

Another excellent focal development technique is to work on your hardest task first. Human nature tends to have us do the easy tasks on our list first because we will feel more accomplished. However, with each task, we make multiple decisions (as small as choosing the font size in an email). With each decision, our brain power and energy is slightly depleted. Thus, by the time you are done with multiple little tasks, you have already lost the focus and brain power to work on the harder task. However, if you get the hard task done first, the little tasks are still easy to do because they are not overwhelming tasks to begin with.

CHAPTER 3

I Am Special

Imagine This: *You and your significant other are planning a vacation. You both agreed to keep the budget of the trip under $2,500 as you are saving for your first home. When your significant other is not around, you call your travel agent and change the budget to $10,000 because you feel you deserve a spectacular vacation. When your significant other finds out, you guilt them into agreeing to take the money out of your house savings so that you can get the vacation you "deserve."*

The above scenario is a bit of an exaggeration but it is an excellent example of the "I Am Special" Syndrome—or Inherent Discrimination as I like to call it—that seems to be plaguing our society today.

> INHERENT DISCRIMINATION: SENSE OF ENTITLEMENT; THE BELIEF THAT ONE IS INTRINSICALLY DESERVING OF PRIVILEGES OR

SPECIAL TREATMENT; AN UNREALISTIC, UNMERITED, OR INAPPROPRIATE EXPECTATION OF FAVORABLE TREATMENT AT THE HANDS OF OTHERS; A.K.A. ENTITLEMENT OR "I AM SPECIAL" SYNDROME

INHERENT: INVOLVED IN THE CONSTITUTION OR ESSENTIAL CHARACTER OF SOMETHING; BELONGING BY NATURE OR HABIT : INTRINSIC

DISCRIMINATION: THE UNJUST OR PREJUDICIAL TREATMENT OF DIFFERENT CATEGORIES OF PEOPLE OR THINGS, ESPECIALLY ON THE GROUNDS OF RACE, AGE, OR SEX; THE PRACTICE OF UNFAIRLY TREATING A PERSON OR GROUP OF PEOPLE DIFFERENTLY FROM OTHER PEOPLE OR GROUPS OF PEOPLE

This topic brings a smile to my face because it brings me back to the 1980s when Janet Jackson came out with a song entitled "What Have You Done For Me Lately?" However, this is nothing to smile about. Entitlement is an attitude that is rampant in our society today, both in our young people and our adults. This is where we are always focused on what people should give us, what the government owes us, what society should provide us, etc.

Why Is Entitlement so Widespread?

More and more psychologists and other experts are studying entitlement in our society today, and according to many there are four cultural trends[13] that have come together to cause this "Entitlement Movement," as many are calling it:

1. **The Self-Esteem Movement:**[14] Since the 1970s, children have been raised with and people in general have been inundated with the "You are special and unique" idea. Everyone has become overly concerned with hurting others' self-esteem. So much so that everyone wins a trophy in Little League, whether they are the winners or losers, students receive higher grades than they deserve, and everyone receives praise rather than constructive criticism—all in the name of not hurting anyone's feelings or self-esteem.

2. **Celebrity Culture:** In today's modern world, our celebrities are reality TV stars who have done nothing that truly warrants being labeled as "famous" other than coming from a "famous" family or doing something notorious that lands them on the news in a shocking scandal. So many of our so-called celebrities are

---

[13] Welch, Kristen. "5 Signs Kids are Struggling with Entitlement." Dec 2013. http://wearethatfamily.com/2013/12/5-signs-kids-are-struggling-with-entitlement/

[14] This movement has its roots in the 1969 book, *The Psychology of Self-Esteem*, by Nathaniel Branden. This book espoused that one must do whatever he/she can to achieve positive self-esteem.

celebrated not for their talents but for their stupidity; not for their accomplishments but for their simply existing. Why work, when you can just be "famous"?

3. **Social Media:** Social media connects us all more than ever, yet it also isolates us behind our computer screens and a layer of fabricated success. We are all so concerned with self-promotion and how we appear to other people that we inflate who we are online. And when we don't get enough "likes" or "retweets" we question who we are and why others don't like us.

4. **Credit Bubble:** Like social media, our real world also lives on comparison—comparison of ourselves to others, their families, their houses, their cars, etc. With the invention of the modern credit card (which first appeared in the 1960s[15]), it has become commonplace to buy things we can not afford because we want them or even "need" them.

Why is it that these four movements have resulted in entitlement? Just think about it. If you are raised knowing you are special and deserve praise no matter how you perform, idolizing celebrities who make enormous profits for doing

---

[15] Boors tin, Daniel. "Credit History: The Evolution of Consumer Credit in America." https://www.bostonfed.org/education/ledger/ledger04/sprsum/cred history.pdf

nothing, worrying more about how you appear to others online and in person than who you really are inside, and knowing you can buy whatever you want as long as you have a piece of plastic with you, how can you not be entitled?

The "I Am Special" Syndrome has infiltrated every level of society and it is something we did to ourselves. I truly believe this is a mentality that needs to change. As in any discrimination, it is disadvantageous to ourselves because we contribute to the decline of society as a whole. Entitlement is robbing us of the skills we need in order to be successful in our lives: responsibility, a work ethic, independence, and self-motivation.

Five Signs of Entitlement

According to Kristen Welch, there are five statements that are signs that a child is suffering from entitlement.[16] Though these statements may seem a little juvenile, I believe the sentiment behind them is the same in adults who are entitled:

1. "I want it now."

2. "I don't want to work for it."

3. "I don't have to clean up my mess."

---

[16] Welch, Kristen. "5 Signs Kids are Struggling with Entitlement." Dec 2013. http://wearethatfamily.com/2013/12/5-signs-kids-are-struggling-with-entitlement/

4. "I want it because everyone else has it."

5. "I expect you to fix all of my problems."

Case Study: Gregg

I once had a client Gregg that came from a well-off family. Throughout Gregg's adolescence and young adulthood, he got into a good amount of trouble: legal issues, minor drug charges, girlfriends that would steal from him, and more. Yet, every time he got into any little bit of trouble, whether it was a parking ticket or something major, he would run to his family to help and they would always help him get out of whatever hot water his poor decisions had gotten him into.

This pattern led to Gregg becoming so entitled that he felt that he could do anything he wanted and not face the consequences. As an adult, Gregg would say whatever he felt to anyone, burning a number of bridges. He would agree to do things one way and then change his mind and do things completely opposite without consulting other parties. If he got flack for his actions or words, he would simply apologize and say that he "didn't mean it that way" or throw his weight around that he was the "boss" and it was an "executive decision."

Thankfully, Gregg's entitlement did not lead to him getting into legal trouble, but it did lead him to ruining numerous relationships in his family, personal life, and professional life. He became known as “flaky” and “selfish” and no one, not even his own family, really trusted him.

When he came to me, Gregg was a mess. His self-esteem was on the floor and he didn’t really have anyone whom he could call a friend or confide in. The onset of our coaching relationship was rough; the first day he was justifying why his life was the way it was and blaming everyone around him. I told him that was utter BS. His life was exactly where it was because of the decisions he had made. He stormed out of my office. I was certain that first coaching session would be our last.

However, never say never. A few days later, Gregg called my office and made another appointment. He came in very humble and said that he agreed with my assessment; that his life was where it was only because of his choices. That first revelation was huge. He finally had owned some of his choices, had taken back some of his power, and had begun to see the world from outside of his personal viewpoint.

From there, we began to further develop his self-awareness. We did a lot of role reversal scenarios, so that he could see how his actions/statements would most likely be interpreted by someone else. We also worked on developing his self-esteem so that he owned his personal power and he did not feel the need to exert his "power" on others.

Within a year of coaching, Gregg was much better. He had been able to repair his relationships with his children and even some of his siblings. He also had a thriving business with employees who trusted him and were loyal to him.

What's Going On

Throughout Gregg's time with me, we worked on what I like to call "Attitude Reformation."

> ATTITUDE REFORMATION: CHANGING ONE'S ATTITUDE FROM ONE OF ENTITLEMENT TO ONE OF GRATITUDE; OWNING THE CONSEQUENCES OF ONE'S ACTIONS; LEARNING TO SEE THINGS FROM ANOTHER'S PERSPECTIVE

> ATTITUDE: A SETTLED WAY OF THINKING OR FEELING ABOUT SOMEONE OR SOMETHING, TYPICALLY ONE THAT IS REFLECTED IN A PERSON'S BEHAVIOR

> REFORMATION: THE ACT OR PROCESS OF IMPROVING SOMETHING OR SOMEONE BY

REMOVING OR CORRECTING FAULTS, PROBLEMS, ETC

Healthy Self-Esteem

Gregg's biggest issue was his low self-esteem, which is something that is rampant with people suffering from "I Am Special" Syndrome. Because people who are extremely entitled choose not to work for things and often do not face any consequences, they have never really developed a strong character within themselves. They have never figured out who they are and what they really want in their lives because whatever their fancy is at that moment, they expect to get it right then and there.

If you are always given everything you want and you never have to delay gratification or work your way up, then you never truly develop as a person. And if you do not develop your view of who you are, you can not have any kind of self-love or self-esteem. To like yourself, you must first know yourself. You must go through various trials and come out on the other side with life lessons that help to define you.

Gregg, like many people, never really had this chance. Thus, that is what we began working on: self-esteem.

In order to stop demanding things and working for them instead, you must have a good sense of who you are. One of the best tools for working on self-esteem is setting goals for yourself that you can accomplish by yourself. Start with small goals first: getting up 30 minutes earlier, taking the stairs instead of the elevator, etc. Every little goal that you set for yourself that you accomplish helps to improve your view of yourself.

Gratitude Bowl

Another great way to develop self-esteem and to dilute the attitude of entitlement is fostering gratitude. When you become grateful for what you already have in your life, you are able to let go of your demands and instead create healthy ambitions for yourself. One of my favorite tools for celebrating what we have in our lives is the Gratitude Bowl.

For this exercise, get yourself a small bowl and some small pieces of paper (sticky notes or halved index cards work well). Each night for 21 days, write one thing down that you are grateful for in your life and place it in the bowl. After 21 days, each morning for another 21 days, take one piece of paper out of the bowl and do something for whatever it is that is written on the paper. For instance, if you had written that you were grateful for your significant other, take them out for an activity that they would enjoy. (Keep in mind the thin line between gratitude and entitlement; make sure it is something *they* would enjoy, not something only *you* enjoy and simply drag them to.) Or if you had written that you are grateful for your home, take time cleaning it yourself that afternoon. Show your gratitude for your life.

Redefine Want vs. Needs

Another really important step to take to combat the feeling of entitlement is to redefine what is a "want" and what is a "need" for you. A need is something that you are entitled to, such as food, water, shelter, a job, transportation, etc. A want is something that you desire but is not required for you to function in your everyday life, such as a meal at an expensive five-star restaurant, rare wine, a mansion, a high-paying job, and a Ferrari. Though all of these examples are really nice things that you may want, they are not necessities. They are luxuries. They are things that you must work for to get and deserve. You have every right to work hard to achieve each and every single one of them and more. And I hope you do, but do not allow yourself to think that you are entitled to them simply because you want them.

When we confuse our wants and needs and give ourselves everything we want we are conditioning ourselves to an entitlement mentality. We are keeping ourselves from developing a work ethic and a strong sense of self to allow us to work for what we want in life. We allow ourselves to become lazy and rob ourselves of becoming the best version of ourselves that we can be.

Change Your View

Another great thing to do is to identify your expectations of yourself, others, the world, etc. Are they realistic? Are they unhealthy? Are they things you can work towards or the demands of a spoiled child? The best thing you can do is to accept life as it is. Do not put unhealthy demands on it that cause you to be disappointed and feel "life isn't fair." Rather, build healthy ambitions for yourself that you can work towards.

Compassion/Empathy

Finally, to really combat any kind of entitlement that you may have allowed into your life, work on developing compassion and empathy for others. Change your view of the word "entitled" and allow yourself to feel "entitled to serve." Take time to serve others. This can be done in any way you choose: volunteering, cooking a nice dinner for loved ones, helping someone with a project, etc. Consciously serving is a humbling experience because you are not performing the action for acknowledgement; you are simply performing the action to help another person out.

Entitlement Is Everywhere

We all have a little entitlement inside of us. It is only human, but it is vital that we keep that entitlement in check by continuously and consciously working on our attitude reformation. Entitlement is one of those sentiments that can take over your entire mindset, if you let it. And when that happens the only person you are really hurting is yourself.

CHAPTER 4

The Secret to Happiness

Imagine This: *You wake up Sunday morning excited. Your busy week is over. You finished all of your chores and errands yesterday. Today is just for you. About an hour or so into the day, you find yourself bored, wondering what you should do. You have a list of to-do's but nothing of want-to's. You're stuck, in a sort of comatose state where you find no motivation to do anything and no drive to work on anything. You turn on your TV and allow yourself to vegetate in order to mute that nagging voice in the back of your mind asking, "Is this all there is?"*

The above scenario is a description of something Austrian neurologist and psychiatrist Viktor Frankl termed "Sunday neurosis." It is, according to Frankl, one of the most common ways an "Existential Vacuum" is discovered in one's life—when the busyness of day-to-day living comes to a halt and you realize that your life has little to no meaning.

This is what I like to call "Substance Abuse."

> SUBSTANCE ABUSE: LACK OF GOALS/MOTIVATION; NOT KNOWING YOUR OWN VALUES OR WHAT YOU STAND FOR; LACKING SUBSTANCE

> SUBSTANCE: THE QUALITY OF BEING MEANINGFUL, USEFUL, OR IMPORTANT; A FUNDAMENTAL OR CHARACTERISTIC PART OR QUALITY

> ABUSE: A CORRUPT PRACTICE OR CUSTOM; IMPROPER OR EXCESSIVE USE OR TREATMENT

That is, your life has no substance. Your life is void of meaning and purpose. In Frankl's most famous book, *Man's Search for Meaning*, he describes a survey he performed that showed that about 60 percent of Americans exhibit a "marked degree of an existential vacuum" in their lives. This book was published in 1946. My guess would be that in today's time that percentage would be much higher.

The Search for Happiness

Why are so many of us lacking meaning in our lives? One reason is the pervasive obsession with happiness. It seems that everywhere you look, you run across someone telling you that you should be happy. That you deserve to be happy. That happiness is the point of life.

There have been a number of studies done on the United States' obsession with happiness. One study showed that people who stated that happiness was their primary goal in life reported 50 percent less frequent positive feelings, 35 percent less life satisfaction, and 75 percent more symptoms of depression than those whose main priority was something other than happiness.[17]

Author Tom Butler-Bowden sums up the problem with focusing on happiness perfectly: "We now live in a world offering endless shortcuts to happiness...But strangely, the easy availability of pleasures tends to leave a yawning hole in many people's lives because it demands zero growth of them as people. A life of pleasures makes us a spectator, not an engager with life. We master nothing and do not use our creativity."[18]

---

[17] Kasdan, Todd. "The Problem with Happiness." *The Huffington Post.* Nov 17, 2011. http://www.huffingtonpost.com/todd-kashdan/whats-wrong-with-happines_b_740518.html.
[18] Butler-Bowden, Tom. *50 Psychology Classics.* Nov 2006.

The Irony of Emotional Favoritism

Interestingly enough, the more a person focuses on being happy the more that focus gets in the way of actually becoming happy. This is because of something that Brené Brown summarizes as "Suppress one emotion, you suppress them all."[19] When we are only focused on positive feelings, we ignore the less pleasant feelings that may be signaling us about situations and circumstances that we may need to address. The irony is that if we were to address these emotions and thus the situations, we would probably be able to find more powerful happiness and meaning in our lives. Instead, we simply allow ourselves to become numb, i.e. the lack of meaning or substance.

Case Study: Bobby

My student Bobby was a star pupil for a long time. He was a very successful writer and changed a lot of people's lives. He was dynamic, successful, and truly content. And then his mother fell very ill and passed away and Bobby fell into a very deep depression for nearly a year and a half.

He stopped working and spent days in his bed just wondering what the point of life was. He tried to be there for his wife and children but found

---

[19] Freedman, Joshua. "Don't Settle for Happiness: Emotional Intelligence and Life Worth Living." *Six Seconds*. Jul 26, 2013. http://www.6seconds.org /2013/07/26/dont-settle-for-happiness/.

himself always hiding away in his own thoughts. He overate and overused prescription medication—anything to numb his pain and his feeling of "nothingness" and utter sadness.

Bobby had every right to mourn his mother's passing and in fact, that is what everyone must do after they lose someone in order to move on with their lives. The problem is that Bobby did not mourn his mother's life, not for the first year of his depression. He did not allow himself to feel the pain. Instead he avoided all feelings and allowed himself to fall into substance abuse (in both the literal meaning and the meaning I use in this chapter).

He'd lost his focus, his meaning, and instead concentrated on his own happiness, or rather the lack of it. When Bobby was finally willing and open to be coached by me again, we spoke frankly. I asked him what his motivation to get up every morning was. He said he didn't have one. He'd lost his life's meaning.

This moment may appear to be the lowest in Bobby's current experience, but it was actually the beginning of his rise out of his depression. By him finally realizing that he was living in a meaningless way and that his mother would not want him to be living in that way, he was able to shock himself out of his comatose state.

The first thing that happened was Bobby truly mourned the loss of his mother. He cried. He felt the despair and the loneliness. He felt the grief. But at least he was finally feeling again.

Little by little we began using simple tools to get Bobby back to living his life. The most important tool we used was having him write down his values—what he stood for, what he lived for, what he longed for, what he wanted. By him doing this, he began to once again see meaning in his life. He began to make plans for the future. He was able to begin opening up to his loved ones and reconnect with them.

Today, Bobby is back to being a very successful writer. I would argue even more successful because he has been able to bring his experience to his work and help others through similar circumstances. Bobby still misses his mother daily, but he is living his life and it is a life of meaning.

What's Going On

The technique that was so effective with Bobby was something I like to call "Motive Profiling."

> MOTIVE PROFILING: FINDING ONE'S GOALS, MOTIVATION, AND/OR DRIVE; KNOWING WHAT ONE STANDS FOR

GOALS: SOMETHING THAT ONE IS TRYING TO DO OR ACHIEVE

DRIVE: A STRONG ORGANIZED EFFORT TO ACCOMPLISH A PURPOSE

When we allow ourselves to fall into substance abuse by either focusing on shortcuts to happiness or focusing on avoiding pain, we lose focus on our life's goals.

We All Have a Meaning

Every single person has a meaning to fulfill while they are on this earth. Each one of us is meant to do something that no one else can do. None of us is meant to live a meaningless existence, yet so many of us do at least in certain moments of our lives. Some out of fear of feeling pain, as Bobby did, some out of fear of the unknown, and some out of knowing nothing better since our society rarely focuses on meaning nowadays.

Too Busy or Unwilling

Some people are not willing to take the time to sit down and really think about not only the direction of their life but also the overall perspective of where they want to get in life. A lot of times they just go week by week, yet they never sit down and say, *"This is where I want my life to be in 6 months or 12 months,"* or any type of time period. Some think, *"Oh I have it up here, all in my head,"* but the actuality is that our plans do not become a reality until we put it on paper. We can toss an idea around in our head for hours, days, or years, but it's never quite as clear as when you see it written down.

To Find Meaning, We Must Take Time to Find Values

Nathaniel Branden, American psychotherapist and writer known for his work in the psychology of self-esteem, argues that true happiness—that is, true meaning—stems from values that have been consciously chosen and developed.

So what are values? Values are the guiding principles of your life and what you stand for. Everyone knows that values are "there;" in some amorphous place, but so many people do not know what they are, or what theirs are, or how to foster them.

Motive Profiling Exercise

Sit down in a quiet place with a journal and pen. Ask yourself: *What do I stand for?* Most people tend to write "family" or "children" first. However, this exercise must go beyond that. This is about you. When people look at you, what do they see? What do you want them to see? What do you stand for?

Move your family out of the way, your children out of the way, and even God, or your Higher Power, out of the way. Reflect on you. Ask yourself: *What am I doing with me? Who am I? What am I sacrificing in my life? My time? My health? My finances?* When you really evaluate where you are sacrificing the most, it will probably point you in the direction of where your compass is pointing; what your values are.

Now ask yourself: *If I keep going in this direction, am I going to get to where I want to go? Am I going to experience the things that I want to? Will it give me the quality of life I want to live? What is the end result of where I am going? Is that something I will be content with when my life is over?*

Find A Coach

If the answer is "No" to the final step in the above exercise, then you need a coach. You need a verifiable coach that can help you structure your life for the next six months, one year, and three years. Look for someone who is successful in the certain area that you want to focus on. If you want to build a business, find an expert in business. If your goal is to live a balanced life of work and play, find someone who is successfully doing that and ask them to mentor you.

No matter what our goals are, we all need coaches or mentors to help us get there. Why? Because it is hard for us to call ourselves out on our own excuses and mistakes. We will always find a justification. We need someone who is not involved in our daily lives as a friend and who can look at the scenarios going on in our lives or the aspects we are questioning from an unbiased outsider's perspective. It is vital to find someone who has the experience, the know-how, and the ability to give unbiased opinions to help us evaluate our lives and our goals successfully.

Benefits of Living Meaningfully

When you begin the awakening process, which is what this book is about, you may stir up a lot of emotions. It may be difficult to first realize that you are not living a very meaningful life or at least not the one you want to be living. You may be tempted to close your eyes to the whole thing and go back to living on a superficial level. Please do not allow fear to keep you from living fully.

According to many different studies, people who live meaningful lives feel more connected to others, to their work, to a life purpose, and to the world itself. There are numerous benefits to living meaningfully, including:

- increased psychological well-being,
- increased creativity, and
- increased work performance.[20]

Living meaningfully allows you to feel whole and to feel you have a purpose. Do not allow fear of the unknown to keep you from finding your meaning and living it. It is a journey worth taking.

[20] Baumeister, Roy F. "What is Better – A Happy Life or a Meaningful One?" *Aeon Essays.* Sept 2013. https://aeon.co/essays/what-is-better-a-happy-life-or-a-meaningful-one

CHAPTER 5

Identity Crisis

Imagine This: *You spend time with your friend who is antisocial. They don't like to go out, but that's okay, neither do you. The next day you are talking to your coworker who loves to go out and have fun. They invite you go out barhopping that weekend. Of course you agree because you love to go out, just like them. That night, at home, you are alone and debating whether you should stay in to eat or go out to eat. Do you prefer to stay in or go out? You're not sure...*

The above scenario is a simple description of what I like to call an "Identity Crisis." The person in the description has no idea what they themselves like to do. They mold their identity to fit those they are around.

> IDENTITY CRISIS: A FEELING OF UNHAPPINESS AND CONFUSION CAUSED BY NOT BEING SURE ABOUT WHAT TYPE OF PERSON YOU REALLY

ARE OR WHAT THE TRUE PURPOSE OF YOUR LIFE IS

IDENTITY: WHO SOMEONE IS; THE NAME OF A PERSON; THE QUALITIES, BELIEFS, ETC., THAT MAKE A PARTICULAR PERSON OR GROUP DIFFERENT FROM OTHERS

CRISIS: A DIFFICULT OR DANGEROUS SITUATION THAT NEEDS SERIOUS ATTENTION

Who Are You?

At some point in each of our lives, we ask ourselves, *"Who am I? Why am I here? What is my purpose?"* These questions are necessary for our growth and our answers may change as we experience our lives. However, the main aspect of ourselves—who we truly are—our identity, is something that is usually molded as children through young adulthood and stays fairly intact. At least, it should if we have had the chance to properly develop our own identity and sense of self.

Honor Yourself

For instance, I am an introvert. This may be surprising considering that I love to go on stage and speak to thousands of people at a time. However, my core base is one of shyness and introversion. When I am not working, I prefer to be with a small group of family and friends who know me well. And even then, I still require my alone time to study and be completely by myself. Though I overcame one of the basic qualities of my identity to become a professional speaker, that piece of my identity is still there and I must honor and accept that.

Stage Theory

Psychologist, Erik Erikson actually coined the term "identity crisis" with his Stage Theory that suggests there are eight different stages that we must pass through as a baby all the way to old age. In each stage we must face a new challenge that we hopefully master. For instance, from birth till about two years of age, Erikson suggests that we go through the "Basic Trust vs. Mistrust" crisis. If we are able to master basic trust, then we develop the virtue of hope. However, if we have not mastered the stage by the time the next one starts (which Erickson based on age), we will supposedly continue to struggle with hope throughout the rest of our lives. (See the Appendix for a full chart of all eight stages.)

I do not necessarily agree with Erikson's theory 100 percent. However, I do believe there is some value in studying it. I do know that those clients of mine who had a very turbulent first few years of their lives do have more trouble developing hope and trust in relationships than others do.

Erikson's theory suggests that we all go through an identity crisis in stage five, which he called "Identity vs. Role Confusion." This stage occurs during adolescence, 13 - 19 years of age and is when we ask, *"Who am I? What can I be?"* Again, this certainly does seem to be the age when we as humans are finally coming into our own identities and trying to figure out who we are, what we stand for, and what we want from our lives.

Role Confusion

However, what happens when we are not able to develop our identity fully during this age? This can happen for a number of reasons, including a dysfunctional family life, low self-esteem, or even just the desire to fit in. In all of these situations, we tend to take on another person's role or views so that we do not have to be our own person, usually because we do not even know who we truly are.

Signs of an Identity Crisis

Harley Therapy has a great summary of seven signs that you may be struggling with your own identity:

1. You change with your environment.

2. Relationships mold you.

3. You often have radical shifts in your opinion.

4. You don't like being asked about yourself.

5. You get bored easily.

6. Your relationships don't run deep.

7. Deep down you don't trust yourself.[21]

We all can suffer from some of these symptoms from time to time. For instance, if you are in an uncomfortable social situation, you may change your opinions slightly to feel more accepted. However, if you change with nearly every situation you are in, then odds are that you really are not quite sure who you are and what you stand for.

Case Study: Kathy

Kathy was a young woman of about 27 when she first came to me for coaching. She had just gotten a divorce and was working for her family's business. She was struggling with severe emotional ups and downs. One minute she would be a professional woman running a meeting and next she would be having an outburst like a 10-year-old

---

[21] *Harley Therapy*. "Help! Who Am I? 7 Signs That You Suffer From an Identity Crisis." May 8, 2014. http://www.harleytherapy.co.uk/counselling/who-am-i-identity-crisis.htm

child throwing a temper tantrum. If you asked her opinion of something, it would mirror those around her or what she thought others might want to hear.

As a child, Kathy did not have it easy. Her mother was an alcoholic and abusive both verbally and physically. Kathy became the main caregiver to her five-year-old sister when she was just 15. She took on the role of the mother and father and made sure that her sister was fed, bathed, clothed, and cared for. She put her needs aside and even cared for her mother who was often passed out.

When I asked Kathy about this time in her life, she usually would say that she was grateful for it. She said had she not had her sister to care for, she probably wouldn't be alive today; that her sister kept her from committing suicide because she had a reason to live.

However, when we delved deeper, we discovered that she also was incredibly resentful of the situation and deep down felt guilty for feeling that way. We discovered that it was this deep-seated resentment and guilt that caused Kathy to have those outbursts. Though it may seem cheesy, it was her inner child screaming for the attention she never had gotten when she was younger.

When I asked Kathy who she was, she couldn't tell me. She could only identify herself as a victim of abuse. It was all she ever seemed to talk about.

Anything that was said she could somehow bring it back to that time for her. She was stuck in a vicious cycle and she knew it.

I had Kathy journal. A lot. She filled almost a journal a month for our first few months of work. One of the most powerful exercises she did was write a letter to her younger self. She wrote a letter of love and understanding to herself. She told herself the positives that came from the experiences and the negatives. She told herself her virtues and her dreams. She told herself who she was during that time in her life.

Little by little, Kathy figured out who Kathy was today. She was able to close the chapter on her abusive childhood and properly put away the inner child that liked to have tantrums. She began to study things she liked and found a job that helped her work on her purpose. When asked who she is now, she says, *“loyal, a caregiver, a protector, independent, professional, intelligent,”* and so much more. She has never forgotten her childhood, but it is not something that she brings up regularly. Now it is just something that happened to her that she is grateful for, because it has made her who she is and she truly likes who she is.

What’s Going On

Kathy went through a number of tools that enabled her to get to know herself. She learned to accept herself as who she was and learned techniques to give herself leeway to make mistakes and to grow. This is what I like to call "Sustainable Strategizing."

> SUSTAINABLE STRATEGIZING: GETTING TO KNOW YOURSELF AND UNDERSTANDING YOUR GOALS; STRATEGIZING YOUR LIFE OR BUSINESS TO ACHIEVE THOSE GOALS; HAVING A PLAN SO THAT YOU ARE NO LONGER CONFUSED

> SUSTAINABLE: ABLE TO BE MAINTAINED AT A CERTAIN RATE OR LEVEL; ABLE TO BE UPHELD OR DEFENDED

> STRATEGY: A CAREFUL PLAN OR METHOD FOR ACHIEVING A PARTICULAR GOAL USUALLY OVER A LONG PERIOD OF TIME; THE SKILL OF MAKING OR CARRYING OUT PLANS TO ACHIEVE A GOAL

Journal Exercise

Everyone says it, but it's true. The first step to any kind of personal growth is to get yourself a journal. You may have a desire to use your computer or your phone, but please consider using a regular journal and a pen or pencil. Psychologically speaking, we respond better when we handwrite our journal entries; especially in the beginning. Your body is fully engaged and it will enable you to go deeper. Not to mention the fact that there is no chance your journal will start to ring or send you a notification of a new email. A paper journal allows you to focus on you, which is the whole point.

Make sure to choose a journal that connects with you. Go to a store and look at a few, touch them, see how the paper feels, etc. Find one that calls to you. Make sure to carry it with you everywhere you go.

For the first 21 days of journaling, follow these steps:

1. **One Page:** For the first week, write an entire page—no more and no less. Every time you sit with your journal, you must write an entire page. You can do as many entries as you want or as few (make sure to at least write one a day). This may seem difficult at first. For some, filling an entire page may seem impossible. For others, filling only a single page may seem too difficult. The reason for this page limit is to force yourself out of your comfort zone and to teach you discipline, consistency, and how to follow directions; not necessarily in that order. For those of you who have trouble finding words, this will force you to dig deep and find the words you need to

express. For those of you who have too many words, this will force you to be selective with what you say and find those words that are really the most important for the situation. Either way, the exercise will begin to help you figure out your true feelings and who you truly are.

2. **Schedule It:** After the first week, set aside time each day. Schedule a time for yourself that you have to journal. Each and every day. Many of my students like to start their days with journaling and end their days with journaling. This does not have to be a long time. Five to ten minutes is all you really need.

3. **Turn Off the Editor:** Remember, no one will be reading this journal but you. Stop criticizing yourself for your handwriting or your spelling or your grammar. Just get the thoughts on the page.

4. **Do Not Limit Yourself:** If you find yourself wanting to journal throughout your day, do not keep yourself from doing so simply because it is not a scheduled time. Write whenever you feel the need to write.

5. **Reread:** At least once a week, go back and reread your entries for the week. Start looking at patterns. Do you always feel a certain way when someone does something specific? Do

you have more effective days when you journal more? There is no right or wrong answer. You are simply getting to know yourself and what the specific life recipes for you are.

6. **Test It Out:** Here's where the strategy comes in. Once you have discovered a life recipe for yourself, you must test it to make sure you understand it. If a certain situation makes you feel a certain way, what can you do to change it? If journaling more makes your day more effective, how does your day change if you schedule an extra journal time for yourself during your lunch break? Have fun with this. See yourself as an experiment that you are testing to get the best results.

7. **Be Patient:** Figuring out your life recipes and learning the best ways to tweak them for you will take some time. It is not something that will happen overnight. Nor are these recipes something that will work forever. As we grow and change, so do our life recipes. But journaling will always be one of the best ways to figure out your current patterns and how to create changes in your personal behavior and development.

Accept Yourself

No matter where you are in the journey of life, stop being so hard on yourself. You are exactly where you are meant to be at the moment you are at. This is your chance to make a change and to move forward with what you want to do. Do not squander it. Accept yourself, love yourself, and push yourself. You are so incredibly worth it.

CHAPTER 6

Human Connection

Imagine This: *You live alone. You work on a computer all day. You communicate via email and text messages mostly. Your social interaction is primarily on social media. When you have to call a utility company to ask a question about your bill, you find yourself dreading making the simple call. You finally force yourself to dial and are met with a robotic voice that greets you with "Thank you for calling. For sales, press 1. For service, press 2..."*

The above scenario is an exaggerated example of "Social Dysfunction." Modern technology and society have made interacting on a human-to-human level almost obsolete, so much so that when we do need to actually speak to someone else, many times we get anxious or just do not know how to act properly.

SOCIAL DYSFUNCTION: AN UMBRELLA TERM USED TO DESCRIBE A VARIETY OF EMOTIONAL PROBLEMS LARGELY EXPERIENCED IN SOCIAL SITUATIONS

Technological Strangers

The amazing rate that technology has interfered in the social interactions between people is astounding in today's world. A decade or so ago, if I was standing in line somewhere, I would strike up a conversation with one of the strangers in the line with me. Now, I simply pick up my cell phone and catch up on social media or text messages. I can't tell you how often I see people out at restaurants all on their phones instead of having actual conversations with each other.

Technology has shifted our society and our views of communication and interaction drastically. We no longer paint the picture; we just take the picture. We do not live through an experience; we want to make sure to capture it and share it with the world. Do not misunderstand me; I believe in capturing moments and sharing moments, but not at the expense of experiencing the moments. There is a fine balance, which many of us are lacking.

Lack of Communication

Do you know your neighbors? I must admit that I don't, but my mother knew her neighbors and knew them well. In today's world, we barely step away from our screens—our phone screens, our computer screens, our television screens—to see who is around us. Modern life gives us so many easy and quick options, but it also gives us a whole lot less opportunities for truly social relationships and interaction.

Fear of Commitment

Things are so easy nowadays that we have all developed a fear of commitment. In fact, many companies have changed their marketing strategies to fit this fear of commitment. You no longer have to commit to a two-year phone contract with a mobile phone company. Now you can get a pay-as-you-go option or even some kind of upgrade plan that lets you change your phone as soon as a new one becomes available.

Avoidance of Conflict

The ease of our modern age also makes avoiding conflict easy. People tend to just walk away from challenges. Everything is so easy, that when anything challenging arises, we don't like it. If we can't point, click, and do, then it's too hard and we just give up. We've lost our work ethic. We've forgotten that it is only through conflict that we grow, push our boundaries, and learn about who we are.

Narcissism and Lack of Skill

We are very self-centered naturally. We tend to always think that people think the same way we do and technology has made us even more self-centered. We are simply not interacting with as many people nor with as many different personalities as we used to. As a result, we have lost some of the skills for learning how to handle different personalities. Instead of learning to embrace and cherish our differences, we run from them and stick to the safety of our technological and isolated bubbles.

Divorce: A Symptom of A Larger Problem

Our society as a whole has become so transient that there is no wonder we are afraid to commit. More than half of all first-time marriages in the United States now end in divorce.[22] There are two different arguments for this statistic: one, people are more afraid of commitment than they used to be and are used to "jumping ship" whenever things get

[22] Twenge, Jean M. "Why Adults Are Less Happy Than They Used to Be." *Psychology Today*. Nov 6, 2015. https://www.psychologytoday.com/blog/our-changing-culture/201511/why-adults-are-less-happy-they-used-be

a little tough; and two, people are yearning for social interaction that they aren't getting elsewhere so they rush into committed relationships before they are ready. Personally, I believe it is a combination of both reasons and I think they both speak volumes about our society as a whole.

Crisis of Loneliness

Here are some stats from a 2012 Badoo Survey:

- 39 percent of Americans spend more time socializing online compared to face-to-face, more than in the U.K. (36 percent) and Germany (35 percent)

- 31 percent admit they sometimes get lonely and 35 percent would like to increase their circle of friends

- Nearly 20 percent prefer communicating online or via text, compared to chatting face-to-face or via phone

- 24 percent have exaggerated or lied about who they've met or what they've done on their social networks[23]

[23] Badoo. 2012. http://www.marketwired.com/press-release/generation-lonely-39-percent-americans-spend-more-time-socializing-online-than-face-1648444.htm

We're all more connected, yet we are more alone than ever before. This isolation is really not good for us. Numerous studies show that feelings of isolation lead to physiological changes within our bodies that lead to illness and even early death.[24] Moreover, studies show that social ties are linked with longer lifespans, decreased stress levels, and increased feelings of well-being overall.[25]

Case Study: Aaron

Aaron was in his early 30s when he came to me. He had severe social anxiety. He had a small tight-knit group of friends, but he barely communicated to others outside of that group. He worked in an office in front of a computer and spent his days plugging away at spreadsheets. He was ghastly afraid of making phone calls. In fact, he once kept his online membership to Netflix for a full year though he didn't use it because he was too scared to pick up the phone and ask customer service to cancel his membership.

Aaron came to me because he found himself feeling unfulfilled. He felt like a robot hiding in his cubicle all day not interacting with anyone. He wanted to do something that fed his creativity and

---

[24] Szalavitz, Maia. "Social Isolation, Not Just Feeling Lonely, May Shorten Lives." *Time*. Mar 26, 2013. http://healthland.time.com/2013/03/26/social-isolation-not-just-feeling-lonely-may-shorten-lives/
[25] Gregoire, Carolyn. "Five Reels for a Happier Life." *The Huffington Post*. Aug 11, 2013. http://www.huffingtonpost.com/2013/08/11/how-this-harvard-psycholo_n_3727229.html

that helped him feel alive. He wanted to feel connected with himself and the world.

We worked on numerous soul-searching techniques to find exactly what it was that Aaron wanted. He soon discovered, or perhaps re-discovered is a better word, that he had a passion for art and sketching that he had allowed to fall by the wayside. Aaron worked out a plan for himself and began applying to part-time jobs in the graphics and arts fields. He soon had a job that allowed him to work around his other job's schedule.

Little by little, Aaron began coming out of his shell. He spent his evenings and weekends with other creative people in an office that had no cubicles. He bonded with his co-workers over their mutual interests. Within six months, Aaron had managed to secure a full-time job as a graphic designer and was able to say goodbye to his technical job.

Today, Aaron is the senior designer at a graphic arts firm. He spends time with coworkers outside of work as well as his original group of friends. He also plays soccer at a neighborhood club one time a week. When I asked him how he feels about speaking to strangers on the phone now, he told me that he still gets nervous but he'll pick up the phone and dial on the first try.

What's Going On

Aaron developed a skill called "cordial diversity" that allowed him to develop relationships with others, which in turn allowed him to become more well-rounded and fulfilled overall.

> <u>CORDIAL DIVERSITY:</u> HAVING THE SOCIAL SKILLS TO COPE WITH VARIOUS PERSONALITY TYPES

By taking another job that forced himself out of his isolated pattern, Aaron opened himself up for change. Because he chose to work in something that he was passionate about, he found it easier to relate with others that had the same passion. As he developed these social skills, he was later able to use them to strengthen his relationships with his older friends, as well as to create new relationships like those with his soccer buddies. His growth was very incremental, but he wanted to change and he did.

Find Your Balance

Technology is amazing. I love it. I'm known as the gadget man in my family. Whenever a new device comes on the market, I'm one of the first persons to get it, but again, everything must be balanced. Technology is wonderful, but so are the people who made it and the people in your life.

Do not forsake the warm-blooded people who have chosen to be a part of your life for that newest app or notification. Six months from now, that device will probably not be as important to you, but the person will be. The question is whether the person you've neglected will still be around six months from now.

Technology is a tool. Not a crutch. Do not use it as a replacement for person-to-person interaction, but rather as a supplement. There's nothing wrong with picking up your phone, but don't do it during dinner. Communicate through social media, but also communicate face to face.

One technique that I use on a regular basis is to take a break from my phone when I am spending time with others. For instance, when a friend comes over, I'll take a photo with them to capture the moment, but then I will turn my phone on silent and set it down away from me. This way I allow myself to grab a memory for the future, yet also allow myself to actually experience the moment while I'm living it too. I have found this to be an excellent way to balance my use of technology.

Embrace Differences

Different personalities are what make our world interesting. They are what add spice and color to our world. Do not allow yourself to be put off by people with different lifestyles, looks, and who make different choices. When you learn to appreciate the variety of personalities in the world, you will see how truly beautiful it is.

So often when we meet someone for the first time, we make subconscious snap judgments about him or her. And then we allow those judgments to keep us from actually getting to know the person. This unconscious behavior robs us of making meaningful human connections more often than we realize.

When we do not like something about someone, it is usually a characteristic within ourselves. It is the reflection of that characteristic back to us that irritates us. Work on you rather than blaming others. Once you work on changing yourself, you will find that you either are no longer bothered by the other person or you at least have sympathy and understanding for them.

Communication Is a Necessity

Many people today may say that they do not need adequate social skills because they spend a lot of time by themselves, work on a computer, or their job does not require them to deal with a lot of people. However, the reality of it is, unless you're living in a bubble, you will eventually have to go to the grocery store, buy a vehicle, have a technician come and install cable, etc. Unless you are living in a very dramatic and unique situation, you can not totally avoid people.

As such, you must develop a certain level of social skills so that you can live your life. We are social creatures and we need social interaction in order to thrive and live fully. Babies need human touch in order to develop. Psychologist Harry Harlow performed a famous experiment in the 1950s that showed that rhesus monkeys preferred to cuddle with a terry cloth covered wire frame that acted as a surrogate mom over drinking milk from a bare wire frame. The monkeys chose love and interaction over food. We are very similar to monkeys in that respect and must remember that social interaction is one of our basic necessities.

Three Types of Social Connectedness

John Cacioppo, a professor of psychology at the University of Chicago, has summarized three types of social connections and interactions. Cacioppo and his team suggest it is important for everyone to work on developing all three in order to fight feelings of loneliness and isolation:

1. "**Intimate Connectedness:** Comes from having someone in your life you feel affirms who you are.

2. **Relational Connectedness:** Comes from having face-to-face contacts that are mutually rewarding.

3. **Collective Connectedness:** Comes from feeling that you're part of a group or collective beyond individual existence."[26]

All three of these areas are important for each of us to live happy, healthy, and full lives. Fill your life with lots of healthy relationships. Find one or two people who truly know you and love you for who you are. Spend time with people who make you happy and make you laugh. And finally, find a group—perhaps an organization with a cause that is near to your heart—that you can be a part of.

By working on all three of these areas, you will find yourself feeling more grounded and centered overall and as most of the studies show, you'll probably live longer too.

---

[26] Bergland, Christopher. "Maintaining Healthy Social Connections Improve Well-Being." *Psychology Today*. Feb 18, 2014. https://www.psychology today.com/blog/the-athletes-way/201402/maintaining-healthy-social-connections-improves-well-being

CHAPTER 7

The Forbidden Topic

Imagine This: *You work at a job that you don't really like and don't really dislike. You're there day in and day out because it pays the bills; well, mostly. Every month you cringe when you look at your statements. You scrimp and save, ask for extensions here and there, and yet still money is always really tight. You've been a loyal employee for years. Those close to you tell you to ask for a raise. But you know you don't deserve it. You don't have the passion you should for your work. And you'd feel guilty if you got a raise anyway. So you just keep dealing with your stress and anxiety each month...*

The above scene is an example of what I like to call "Capital Punishment," where we don't think we're worthy of earning more money and we actually feel guilty about the money we earn.

<u>CAPITAL PUNISHMENT:</u> HAVING NEGATIVE THOUGHTS ABOUT MONEY; PUNISHING ONESELF FOR WANTING MONEY OR LACK OF MONEY; AN UNHEALTHY RELATIONSHIP WITH MONEY

<u>CAPITAL:</u> WEALTH IN THE FORM OF MONEY OR OTHER ASSETS OWNED BY A PERSON OR ORGANIZATION OR AVAILABLE OR CONTRIBUTED FOR A PARTICULAR PURPOSE SUCH AS STARTING A COMPANY OR INVESTING

<u>PUNISHMENT:</u> SUFFERING, PAIN, OR LOSS THAT SERVES AS RETRIBUTION

In fact, modern-day psychology has actually coined a term and a syndrome for these feelings: Sudden Wealth Syndrome. This is described as "excessive guilt for something an individual doesn't believe they're entitled to."[27]

Forbidden Topic

Money is one of those forbidden topics. Along with politics and religion, you're not supposed to

[27] "The Effect of Money on Your Emotions." *Society for Personality and Social Psychology*. 1 Apr 2015. http://www.spsp.org/effect-money-your-emotions

talk about money in most settings. At least, that is what I have always been told. I guess it's because so many of us have such a charged and difficult relationship with money. Those of us who do not have it tend to envy those of us who do have it. And those of us who do have it tend to want to keep it for ourselves rather than share it with others.

Past Connections

Many of us have negative feelings towards money due to the way we were raised or societal views. If there's one person that shouldn't have any money in this world according to how and where that person grew up, then that person would have to be me. I grew up in Little Havana, the inner city of Miami. I remember our first apartment didn't even have its own bathroom; we shared it with everyone on the same floor. I had to be careful putting on my shoes so scorpions that loved to hide in them wouldn't bite me. I was the child of a single, immigrant woman who didn't speak the language and had no one to turn to. No opportunities were waiting for us; we had to fight for everything we needed. I think that upbringing would classify me or label me as a person that should never acquire any successes in their life by many people's standards.

I realized my surroundings and these so-called labels very early in my life. I heard from neighbors that if you were meant to be rich, you would have been born rich. And really, only evil people had money anyway. Good people wouldn't keep money for themselves because then they would be selfish.

However, I would go with my mom to clean affluent homes in good neighborhoods, so I knew there was something better out there. I soon began to recognize the education levels of those around me and saw how their education pretty much determined their lifestyle. Real opportunities for growth, real opportunities to change your life don't come by as easily for those people who grew up in the neighborhoods I did.

Wealth Guilt

You may not have grown up in a similar situation to me. You may have grown up in a wealthy home or a very poor home or somewhere in between. However, no matter where or how you grew up, I bet you have at least some wealth guilt that kicks in from time to time. For the most part, this seems to have become a systemic part of our society. Our television shows and movies always seem to depict the wealthy as the evil ones who are power hungry and dangerous, and the poor as the pure of heart. Wanting money is not a worthwhile goal and makes you "less than" somehow.

Money Focus

However, focusing on money as your sole goal isn't very good either. I believe that we need to be focused on our finances because we only attract what we focus on. However, if you are only worried about making money and not finding and fulfilling your life's purpose, you will always be lacking in your life. You may have all the money in the world, but without living to your full potential, your wealth won't mean very much. In fact, numerous people suffer from a type of capital punishment where they force themselves into jobs they hate in order to make money only to discover that they are truly unhappy.

Case Study: Sarah

Sarah came to me as a coaching student who had always wanted to be an artist. She actually went to college to study art but changed her major midway to accounting because she was worried she wouldn't be able to support herself. Upon graduating, she got a job with an excellent accounting firm and made an extremely good living, but she was terribly unhappy.

Sarah and I worked together for a good two years. First, we worked on figuring out why she was unhappy. Through our coaching sessions, Sarah realized that she felt unfulfilled. Her bank account was full, but her accounting job didn't excite the creative parts of her and left her little time for creative work on the side. I suggested she work at the accounting firm part time and begin working as a freelance graphic artist.

She was excited by the idea but was scared to take the leap. What if she failed? Who was she to turn down a great job to do something artsy? Moreover, she couldn't ask to be paid for her artwork; it was something she loved. If she chose to get paid for it, wouldn't it become a job and then she'd hate that too?

Sarah's underlying issue was a deep-rooted feeling of unworthiness. She didn't feel that she was important enough to actually stand up for herself and say what she wanted. She had always toed the line—done what she was supposed to do—she didn't have the right to want to be happy.

Over our couple of years together, we worked on her self-esteem and self-worth. Sarah finally came to realize that she did deserve to be happy. If she didn't put herself first, she would be full of resentment and anxiety and would never be the best version of herself for anyone.

She also finally began to do freelance work on the side. She wasn't willing to cut her hours at the accounting firm, so she worked on less sleep for the first six months. However, when she began to realize that she could make a good living doing freelance work and not hate it—that she was okay with making less money doing something she truly enjoyed and felt good doing—she finally cut her hours at the accounting firm back little by little until she was only doing artwork.

What's Going On

By working on Sarah's self-esteem and self-worth, we worked on her mindset of "Economic Growth."

> ECONOMIC GROWTH: CHANGING THE NEGATIVE THOUGHTS ONE HAS REGARDING MONEY; REALIZING ONE DESERVES MONEY AND SHOULDN'T FEEL GUILTY FOR WANTING OR HAVING IT; MOREOVER, THAT ONE CAN MAKE MONEY DOING WHAT THEY LOVE/WANT, NOT WHAT THEY OR SOMEONE ELSE THINKS THEY "SHOULD" DO

Sarah began to realize that money isn't everything, but it is a useful tool. She began to see that she deserved to make money doing what she loved to do.

Change Your Mindset

Here's the thing that no one seems to understand. Money is truly an unlimited resource. Unlike water or oil or even air, as T. Harv Ecker says in his book *The Millionaire Mindset*, they just keep printing more money. Just because you earn money doesn't mean someone else has to go without it, so get that limiting thought out of your head. There is truly enough to go around the entire world again and again.

So stop feeling unworthy and start attracting what you deserve to earn into your life. Do not wish harm to or be envious of those who have more than you; instead, learn from them. Ask them to sit down with you and explain how they have earned what they have. Ask them to share their wealth of knowledge. Most everyone will gladly share their time and knowledge with you; you just have to have the courage to ask.

Make Money Doing What You Love

In my early 20s, a friend of mine handed me a book, *Think and Grow Rich* by Napoleon Hill, and I discovered a new way of thinking, a new way of living, and the door to a career that would change my life and my family's life. Soon after, I got a job working for Xerox and I was introduced to the world of professional speaking, as well as a world of teachers and leaders that taught new thinking strategies. And that's where my hunt began. I started looking for more people on the same success path as me. I tried to align myself with people that had similar thought processes and began learning my craft.

This is where I thought I had to work really hard to get what I wanted because that is what people always say. I began working 14, 16, and 18-hour days. From one job to another; opening up businesses, creating new ideas, hunting for that better life. It wasn't until my late 20s, after almost a decade of searching for the pot of gold at the end of the rainbow, that I realized that is not how you attain a different type of lifestyle. I had misunderstood what my relationship with money was.

I discovered that I needed to choose one thing. One thing I loved and was good at and focus on that. For me, this was speaking and personal coaching. If you focus on your niche, you will become rich. This is because you bring passion to your niche that you don't to the other things that you do. And when you work passionately, with finances as part of your goals, you will make money. The trick is to find what you love to do and then figure out how to make money doing it.

Don't Put All Your Eggs in One Basket

I've made millions and lost millions multiple times in our unpredictable economy these past few decades. The problem was that I was so focused on my niche I never protected myself or learned how to properly invest my money.

I didn't understand investments, insurance, real estate, diversification, multiple streams of income, and residual income; all terms that if you don't know, you need to research intensively. My recommendation is to find people in each of these areas, interview them, dissect the information, and find out how you can implement these things into your own life immediately.

Being the son of an immigrant woman with limited education, growing up having no mentors or elders to guide me, I missed a big portion of what would have made my life and career path a lot easier and more stable. However, now as a father, I am trying to make sure that my children understand these things early on so that their challenges are minimized.

Though I recommend focusing on your niche, do not allow yourself to get tunnel vision. No matter how good you are at what you do and how great your income is, there will more than likely be a time when things aren't so great for you. Thus, keep focusing on your niche, but make sure you have a good investment plan in place as well. Make sure that you are putting your money in multiple places and have multiple streams of income. It's important to protect yourself these days.

Relationship With Your Finances

A relationship with your finances is one of the most important relationships that you will have in your life because it determines the quality of your life and how you handle the challenges you sometimes face with those that you love.

A lot of people don't really know where they stand financially and they throw their money all over the place instead of working on one financial solution that is going to move them up in life. Some people will make investments and not really look at them or trust people with their money and not realize that it is their money and they need to manage it more personally.

There are also a lot of people who try to scrape by and they put their money into vices like gambling, drinking, drugs, women, partying, beauty, etc. It's okay to let yourself enjoy some things every now and then but I have seen too many people that constantly say that they are low on money but they go to every sporting event, spend lots of money on their nails or hair, or are living beyond their means. Moreover, sometimes it's not even that people are living above their means but their means have diminished, so they have to reevaluate their expenses consistently.

Money is Energy

It's time we realize that money is energy. We must allow it to flow in order for us to get more. We should neither grasp it so hard that we stop it nor should we let it go anywhere it wants. We must learn how to direct the flow of money.

The biggest issue that we have to face is changing our view of money. So many of us believe that we don't deserve money and so even when we have it we will do everything we possibly can subconsciously to not keep it.

Your Beliefs Equal Your Wealth

Just know that the basis of wealth, as with anything in life, is your own personal mindset and your beliefs. What you focus on will become your reality. Thus, if you focus on not being able to pay your bills, then you will continue to not be able to pay your bills. If you focus on wanting to have just enough to get by, then you will have just enough to get by and not a penny more. However, if you focus on creating a quality of life for yourself and your family that affords you the ability to truly enjoy life and the people in it, then you will attract that into your life as well.

Rich vs. Poor

Rich people work just as hard as, if not harder than, poor people, yet it is their mindset that sets them apart. Poor people focus on their problems while rich people focus on solutions. Poor people focus on what they do not have while rich people focus on what they have. Poor people tend to be more negative while rich people tend to be more positive. These are all generalizations, but if you do your own personal informal survey of the wealthier people you know versus the less wealthy people you know, you will start to see that these generalizations are based on fact.

Take Action

Once you are able to change your mindset and your relationship with money, you will start to attract more of it into your life. Do not misinterpret what I am saying—you can not simply sit meditating on positivity and attracting wealth into your life all day and expect to become obscenely rich. However, your mindset is where it all starts. When you go to work in a positive frame of mind you will be more likely to see opportunities that you would otherwise miss.

Stop punishing yourself for the money you have earned or want to earn. Instead, change your view and open yourself up to economic growth. I have a lot of students who feel that they don't deserve to charge for their services; that it's somehow wrong to get paid for what they do. Why is it that society has taught us that asking to be paid is somehow beneath us?

Let me tell you something, no one is going to hand you anything in this world. Most people will not pay you unless you ask, but you do deserve to be paid for whatever it is that you do. Asking to be paid is not something to shy away from or to feel badly about; it is part of the process. You are asking to be recognized for the good work that you are doing and that is only right.

I have helped and plan to continue to help a lot of people in my life. I have done thousands of hours of personal and business coaching with students from all walks of life—from dog walkers to CEO's of multi-million dollar companies—and I have been paid by each and every one of these students. My rate is not cheap, but it is reasonable. It is what I deem my time worth because I know that what I do helps those who apply what I teach.

Splurge Account

One tool that works really well for developing your responsibility with money is opening what I call a "Splurge Account." This is a separate bank account in which you put away 10 percent of your earnings each month. This is not meant to be savings for a rainy day or extra money for bills.

Instead, this is money that you are allowed to use solely to “splurge” on yourself.

However, you can only use this money to “splurge” on yourself; no other money. For instance, if there is a new cell phone that you want to purchase, but there is not enough money in your Splurge Account, then you can not purchase it yet. Instead, you must wait until you have enough money saved. When this happens, one of two things will occur. One, by the time you have the money saved, your urge to purchase the phone may have subsided, which means it would have just been an impulse buy. Or two, you will purchase the phone and feel even more satisfied with your spending because you truly earned it.

By using the Splurge Account, you will develop a real relationship with your money. You will respect it more, as well as the time and effort it takes to make it.

Time Worth Exercise

Method One – Budget:

1. Add up all of your monthly expenses, including bills, food, fun, etc.

2. Divide that number by 4 (the usual number of weeks in a month).

3. Divide that number by 40 (the usual number of hours a person works in a week).

4. The number you have is the minimum amount you can work for per hour.

Method Two – Your Goal:

1. What is your goal yearly salary?

2. Take that number and divide it by 52 (the number of weeks in a year).

3. Divide that number by 40 (the usual number of hours a person works in a week).

4. The number you have is the minimum amount you can work for per hour.

Now that you know how much your time is worth, does it seem as hard to ask someone to pay you a fraction of that? Do you feel that you deserve to be paid more than that? You have taken the first step. You finally see your worth.

CONCLUSION

Thank you for sharing this journey with me. In all these chapters you may have associated your negative thinking with the beginning of each chapter. You may have been able to recognize some things that you're doing, saying, or believing in your life. My hope is that you can recondition yourself using some of the positive techniques we have outlined in the second section of each chapter.

None of this works overnight. Some of this can take months or even years, but this restructuring is not impossible to do. You're going to have your challenges and you're going to have your successes. With every challenge I hope that you learn a lesson that moves you closer to your successes. I hope that every challenge teaches you something that will elevate you in your journey.

This is a seven-step journey to changing your quality of life. I do recommend that you find experts in each one of the positive aspects outlined in this book to help you grow. Some people think that finding one mentor is the solution for everything but I recommend that you find a mentor for each of the seven positive sides for reconditioning your mind for your life. Remember, "Don't Drink the Koolaide, Think RED."

If you found this book helpful, please share it with others. A book is only as powerful as the number of people it reaches. And please reach out, connect with me on your favorite social media platform, and share your thoughts about this book with me (use the hashtag #IThinkRED). I would love to hear your experiences and your opinions.

Live Life, Don't Let Life Live You!

Bert Oliva

NOTES

CHAPTER 1

Notes for The Walking Dead

CHAPTER 2

Notes for Squirrel Effect

CHAPTER 3

Notes for
I Am Special

CHAPTER 4

Notes for The Secret to Happiness

CHAPTER 5

Notes for Identity Crisis

CHAPTER 6

Notes for Human Connection

CHAPTER 7

Notes for The Forbidden Topic

APPENDIX

Erik Erikson's Stages of Psychosocial Development

Approx. Age	Virtues	Psychosocial crisis	Significant relationship	Existential question	Examples
0-2 years	Hope	Basic trust vs. mistrust	Mother	Can I trust the world?	Feeding, abandonment
2–4 years	Will	Autonomy vs. shame and doubt	Parents	Is it okay to be me?	Toilet training, clothing themselves
4–5 years	Purpose	Initiative vs. guilt	Family	Is it okay for me to do, move, and act?	Exploring, using tools or making art
5–12 years	Competence	Industry vs. inferiority	Neighbors, school	Can I make it in the world of people and things?	School, sports
13–19 years	Fidelity	Identity vs. role confusion	Peers, role model	Who am I? Who can I be?	Social relationships
20–39 years	Love	Intimacy vs. isolation	Friends, partners	Can I love?	Romantic relationships
40–64 years	Care	Generativity vs. stagnation	Household, workmates	Can I make my life count?	Work, parenthood
65-death	Wisdom	Ego integrity vs. despair	Mankind, my kind	Is it okay to have been me?	Reflection on life

Source: https://en.wikipedia.org/wiki/Erikson%27s_stages_of_psychosocial_development

GLOSSARY

9-5 Mentality: in today's society, we have the ability to get caught up in the everyday routines of life, or what we like to call the "9-5 mentality;" a.k.a. "the vicious cycle"

Abuse: a corrupt practice or custom; improper or excessive use or treatment

Affirmative Conditioning: self-thinking; thinking for one's self; forming one's own opinions, and not borrowing them ready-made from others, or merely following prevalent fashions of thought; of independent judgment

Attention Deficit: a disorder in which someone (such as a child) has problems with learning and behavior because of being unable to think about or pay attention to things for very long; a.k.a. "Squirrel Effect"

Attention: the act or power of carefully thinking about, listening to, or watching someone or something; notice, interest, or awareness

Attitude Reformation: changing one's attitude from one of entitlement to one of gratitude; owning the consequences of one's actions; learning to see things from another's perspective

Attitude: a settled way of thinking or feeling about someone or something, typically one that is reflected in a person's behavior

Automaton: a person or animal that acts in a monotonous, routine manner, without active intelligence

Capital Punishment: having negative thoughts about money; punishing oneself for wanting money or lack of money; an unhealthy relationship with money

Capital: wealth in the form of money or other assets owned by a person or organization or available or contributed for a particular purpose such as starting a company or investing

Conditioning: the act or process of training a person or animal to do something or to behave in a certain way in a particular situation

Cordial Diversity: having the social skills to cope with various personality types

Crisis: a difficult or dangerous situation that needs serious attention

Discrimination: the unjust or prejudicial treatment of different categories of people or things, especially on the grounds of race, age, or sex; the practice of unfairly treating a person or group of people differently from other people or groups of people

Drive: a strong organized effort to accomplish a purpose

Economic Growth: changing the negative thoughts one has regarding money; realizing one deserves money and shouldn't feel guilty for wanting or having it; moreover, that one can make money doing what they love/want, not what they or someone else thinks they "should" do

Focal Development: fostering attention or focus

Focus: a main purpose or interest

Goals: something that one is trying to do or achieve

Identity Crisis: a feeling of unhappiness and confusion caused by not being sure about what type of person you really are or what the true purpose of your life is

Identity: who someone is; the name of a person; the qualities, beliefs, etc., that make a particular person or group different from others

Inherent Discrimination: sense of entitlement; the belief that one is intrinsically deserving of privileges or special treatment; an unrealistic, unmerited, or inappropriate expectation of favorable treatment at the hands of others; a.k.a. Entitlement or "I Am Special" Syndrome

Inherent: involved in the constitution or essential character of something; belonging by nature or habit : intrinsic

Motive Profiling: finding one's goals, motivation, and/or drive; knowing what one stands for

Punishment: suffering, pain, or loss that serves as retribution

Reformation: the act or process of improving something or someone by removing or correcting faults, problems, etc.

Social Dysfunction: an umbrella term used to describe a variety of emotional problems largely experienced in social situations

Strategy: a careful plan or method for achieving a particular goal usually over a long period of time; the skill of making or carrying out plans to achieve a goal

Substance Abuse: lack of goals/motivation; not knowing your own values or what you stand for; lacking substance

Substance: the quality of being meaningful, useful, or important; a fundamental or characteristic part or quality

Sustainable Strategizing: getting to know yourself and understanding your goals; strategizing your life or business to achieve those goals; having a plan so that you are no longer confused

Sustainable: able to be maintained at a certain rate or level; able to be upheld or defended

Walking Dead: a person who moves very slowly and is not aware of what is happening especially because of being very tired; a person held to resemble the so-called walking dead (a zombie); especially : automaton

INDEX

9-5 Mentality, 15, 123
Abuse, 54
Action, 100
Affirmative Conditioning, 26, 123
Attention, 30, 32, 36, 123
Attention Deficit, 30, 32, 123
Attitude, 47, 124
Attitude Reformation, 47, 124
Automaton, 16, 124
Awareness, 28
Balance, 83
Beliefs, 99
Branden, Nathaniel, 42, 60
Brown, Brené, 56
Cacioppo, John, 86
Capital, 88, 89, 124
Capital Punishment, 88, 89, 124
Celebrity Culture, 42
Change, 51, 95
Coach, 61
Commitment
  Fear Of, 78
Communication, 2, 77, 85
Compassion, 51
Conditioning, 26, 27, 124
Conflict
  Avoidance Of, 78
Cordial Diversity, 83, 124
Credit Bubble, 43
Crisis, 65, 80, 124
Differences, 84
Discrimination, 41, 125
Divorce, 79
Drive, 59, 125
Ecker, T. Harv, 95
Economic Growth, 94, 125
Emotional Favoritism, 56
Empathy, 51
Energy, 99
Entitlement, 41, 42, 44, 52
Erikson, Erik, 66
Focal Development, 35, 36, 38, 125
Focus, 31, 36, 37, 92, 125
Forbidden Topic, The, 88, 89
Frankl, Viktor, 53
Goals, 59, 125
Gratitude, 49
Happiness, 28, 55, 56
Happiness, Secret To, 53
Human Behavior, 1

Human Connection, 76, 85
I Am Special Syndrome, 40, 41, 44, 126
Identity, 64, 65, 67, 68, 115, 125
Identity Crisis, 64, 67, 68, 125
Signs Of, 67
Inherent, 40, 41, 126
Inherent Discrimination, 40, 48, 126
Journal, 71
Life Recipes, 74
Living Meaningfully, 62
Loneliness, 80
Man's Search For Meaning, 54
Meaning, 59, 60
Millionaire Mindset, The, 95
Mindset, 95
Money, 89, 92, 95, 99
Motive Profiling, 58, 60, 126
Multitasking, 36
Myelin, 18, 19
Narcissism, 79
Negative Thinking, 26, 104
Negativity Bias, 11
Neurons, 17, 20
Neuroplasticity, 17, 21
Passion, 37
Pomodoro Technique, 36
Punishment, 89, 126
Rational Educated Decisions, 12
Reformation, 47, 126
Role Confusion, 67
Self-Esteem, 42, 48
Self-Esteem Movement, 42
Social Connectedness, 86
Social Dysfunction, 76, 126
Social Media, 43
Squirrel Effect, 29, 30, 37, 109, 123
Stage Theory, 66
Strategy, 71, 126
Substance, 54, 126, 127
Substance Abuse, 54, 126
Sudden Wealth Syndrome, 89
Sustainable, 71, 127
Sustainable Strategizing, 71, 127
Technology, 2, 77, 83, 84
Think And Grow Rich, 95
Values, 60
Vicious Cycle, 15, 70, 123
Visualization, 27
Walking Dead, 14, 15, 16, 28, 107, 111, 113, 115, 117, 119, 127
Walking Dead:, 16
Want Vs. Needs, 50
Wealth, 89, 91, 99
Wealth Guilt, 91
Worth, 56, 102

ABOUT BERT OLIVA

Bert Oliva is CEO/Founder of BOWAworld, an international training and development organization that includes seminars, professional coaching, keynotes, and corporate trainings. Some of his clients have included: HBO, Perry Ellis, HP, Marriott IVC, Trump Network and many more. By studying four dimensional concepts—physical, emotional, logical, and spiritual—Bert has been able to develop his basic and fundamental teaching programs into what is today known as "Humanology," the scientific study of Human Potential.

He is known for his success as a corporate coach, sales visionary, consultant, speaker, and entrepreneur. Bert brings real-world advice, carefully researched facts, memorable humor, and powerful stories to the platform in order to shake up, wake up, and motivate audiences in ways that produce lasting results.

Bert speaks from a lifetime of accomplishments and first-hand experience. Drawing on his own experiences and continuous research, Bert offers a wealth of insight into setting yourself apart or creating the right impact anywhere you go. He offers strategies to motivate you to action, improve your performance, relationships, and ability to think in new and creative ways.

To learn more about Bert Oliva, his coaching, or speaking, please visit http://www.BertOliva.com.

Made in the USA
Columbia, SC
26 April 2019